# A Commando

CW00504515

## A son's tribute to his father

By

# Robert Cubitt

© **2018**

Published by Selfishgenie Publishing, England.

# Other titles by the Same Author

**Fiction**
The Deputy Prime Minister
The Inconvenience Store
The Charity Thieves

**Warriors Series**
The Warriors: The Girl I Left Behind Me
The Warriors: Mirror Man

**The Magi Series**
The Magi
Genghis Kant (The Magi Book 2)
New Earth (The Magi Book 3)
Cloning Around (The Magi Book 4)
Timeslip (The Magi Book 5)
The Return Of Su Mali (The Magi Book 6)
Robinson Kohli (The Magi Book 7)
Parallel Lines (The Magi book 8)

**Non-Fiction**
I'm So Glad You Asked Me That
I'm So Glad You Asked me That Again
I Want That Job

# Contents

# Dedication

In loving memory of my father, Robert (Bob) Cubitt.

1927 - 2011

Middlesex Regiment and No 3 Commando.

# Acknowledgements

This book has been a challenge to write and much of it wouldn't exist at all without the generous help given to me by others; some relatives, others complete strangers. I am therefore grateful for that help and would like to take this opportunity to thank the following (in alphabetical order):

My cousin Brian Chalk who is the family genealogist and who provided several of the photographs used; Gary Cruden of the Evening Express; Simon Flavin of Reach Publishing Services; Mark Leventhal of Greenhill Books; Peter Rogers of the Commando Veterans Association; Raphael Smid of bunkerpictures.nl; Sebastian Wainwright of the Imperial War Museum.

Finally I would like to thank those former members of the commandos, without whose reminiscences this book could never have been written.

# Cover Images

The cover images are by my sister, Di Cubitt and were created from photographs in the family collection. They are titled "The Briefing" and "Departures".

My sister is a visual artist originally from the U.K., living in Perth, Western Australia since the nineties. She worked as a glass artist for 14 years in Fremantle before studying fine arts at Curtin University (painting major), graduating with honours in 2007. Since then she has been exhibiting regularly with three solo shows, and participation in over 40 group shows, invitation and selected art awards (for full details see CV page). She has been selected as a finalist in the Albany Art Prize, Royal Perth Art prize for Landscape, 2017 and 2018 and is represented in Perth by Stala Contemporary. She currently works in the School of Art at Curtin University as an art technician and drawing lecturer.

To find out more about Di Cubitt and to see some of her other work, use this link to her website. **http://www.dicubitt.com/about/**

# Sketch Maps

The sketch maps were produced by Uche Onyeabo.

# Foreword

In 1938, my father enlisted in the British Army, joining his local regiment, the Middlesex (Duke of Cambridge's Own). He remained a soldier until 1961, when he retired and found new employment in civilian life. He didn't talk much about the war in which he fought; his generation weren't the boastful type.

But when the Aunties and Uncles gathered at Christmas or other holidays, stories from the war years would be told. They weren't about fighting and bravery, but more about the disruption to daily life, air raids, rationing and the human cost of war. They also talked about the good times; the camaraderie, the spirit of the people, the dances and the songs. At times it sounded like it might have been fun though, of course, it wasn't. As a child I sat in the corner, hardly noticed, and listened as the stories were told. From time to time I heard the word 'Commando' uttered but paid it no particular attention.

There were few small boys growing up in the 1950s and 60s that didn't know about the Commandos, the elite fighting force formed during the Second World War that took the fight across the North Sea and the English Channel, to Africa, to Italy and to the Far East. Comic books were written about these heroes and their deeds and I was an avid fan, spending my pocket money on every edition as it appeared in the newsagents. But I never associated the word with my father, at least not for many years. The comic books were works of fiction; but the truth was often more remarkable.

I knew Dad was a soldier of course. My Mum, my elder sister and me and, in turn, my younger sisters had followed my Dad around the world, travelling as far as Malaya (as it was then) before returning once again to Britain. But that word Commando kept on cropping up and the penny did eventually drop that it was my Dad that they were talking about. Well, him and his mates. Yes, my Dad was one of those legendary heroes.

Getting Dad to talk about his war was like getting blood from a stone. As I said, his generation weren't the boastful types and my father was one of the most modest men I have ever known. I extracted little bits here and there, but never from his own experiences. I heard about Dieppe (Operation Jubilee), but as a battle that was observed rather than participated in. Similarly I heard about D Day (Operation Overlord), as if any of my generation hadn't already seen the film The Longest Day! But what my Dad actually did was always a mystery.

However, it didn't remain so. Eventually I started to read the books that Dad had bought on the subject over the years. One in particular stood out. It was called, simply, "Commando" and had been written by Brigadier John Durnford-Slater, DSO & Bar. The Brigadier had been the first commanding officer of No 3 Commando and this book told their story, from their formation in 1940 through to their disbandment in 1945. At once I realised I had struck gold, because this was my Dad's unit. If he wouldn't tell me what he had done during the war, then the good Brigadier would.

Soon after that I borrowed another book, "Storm From The Sea" by Peter Young. In 1943 he took over command of 3 Commando from Brigadier Durnford-Slater, giving me two sources of information.

However, it was a museum that finally allowed me to hear my father's stories in his own words. In 1996 Dad paid a number of visits to the National Army Museum to record his memories of his army life, as part of the museum's 'audio history' project. He was given copies of the tapes and in 2017 they came into my hands.

As I listened to the tapes they excited the writer in me. I felt that Dad's story needed to be told. Not just for him, or for my family, but for the families of all the men of the Army Commandos. My father and his pals didn't regard themselves as being anything special, but they did some very special things.

Reading Brigadier Durnford-Slater's and Brigadier Peter Young's accounts of various operations it became clear that without the Commandos several of them might not have been quite so successful and some might even have failed. It also made me realise that I was lucky to be here, because casualty rates among the commandos ran at about one in every three soldiers. My Dad was one of the lucky ones that made it through the war relatively unscathed.

So, this is what this book is all about. In each chapter I'll record my father's words, just as he said them. There is some minor editing but only to allow the story to flow a little better. What you will read is what he said.

Information in brackets is supplied by me to clarify something my father has said. I have, very occasionally, re-ordered some of the story to allow for the original interviewer having asked my father to go back to elaborate on something he said earlier. Where this has been done I have indicated it by putting this […] symbol at the start and end of the re-ordered passage. The punctuation is all my own as my father's narrative doesn't allow for the precise interpretation of phrases, sentences and paragraphs.

In the second half of each chapter, I've attempted to put Dad's story into its historical context, telling more about the operations in which he took part; what their aims were, what happened and what they achieved or, occasionally, failed to achieve.

This isn't the story of the Army Commandos. That has been told by better historians than me and you can find my other sources in the bibliography at the end of the book. This is the story of just one of those soldiers that served in the units that were first awarded the accolade of the green beret, which is still worn today by their successors, the Royal Marine Commandos.

This year marks the eightieth anniversary of my father's enlistment into the army and I can think of no better tribute to him than to record his memories of that time of his life. If you sense a little hero worship in what you read, then I plead guilty but I don't apologise. They were all heroes.

# Preface by Brigadier Durnford-Slater DSO & Bar

## (From his book "Commando")

The officers and men of No 3 Commando, like all the army Commandos, were volunteers who were prepared to take their chances. Some got away with it and some did not. They all took plenty of chances.

What were the driving motives behind it all? In the beginning there was a fascination of the unknown. They were taking on a new phase of warfare against the unbeaten German army. The excitement of it all appealed to everybody. There was the happiness of working in good company, with picked volunteers in a star unit. Later, pride in the unit and in the traditions of early operations took the place of novelty and excitement. By 1943 all had their fill of excitement. They were always chosen for the most hazardous operations, and they appreciated the compliment.

Above all there was the satisfaction of doing a good job for a great King, who had visited and encouraged us in our early days.

In their five years of operations, No 3 Commando had their full share of triumph and disaster. Directly one operation was finished, planning started for the next one. Casualties were many and this has never ceased to horrify me.

The Commando tradition of always maintaining the impetus of the advance lasted to the end.

John Durnford-Slater
Bedford
January 1953

Extracted with the kind permission of Greenhill Books.

# 1 – Early Life

I came from a very working-class family, born and bred in Fulham, actually. Things weren't going too well. I'd had a few spats at home, I was unemployed at the time, I decided I would join the army and I went round to join. To my dismay, when I got round there, I found I wasn't actually old enough to join the army.

But two days later, the Recruiting Officer got in touch with me and said "We can take you into the army now, we can take you in onto what we call a supplementary reserve engagement." Which at that time was 6 months training with the colours * and then four years on reserve.

So from there the local man sent me up to Whitehall, I went up to Whitehall, and was very amazed to find that the very day I got there I was given the amazing sum of about three (shillings) and sixpence (about eighteen pence (£0.18)). Which was the King's Shilling ** and a day's subsistence allowance, having been accepted.

Then I had to report to New Scotland Yard as it was in those days, every two days, for which I received two days subsistence, and they occupied us for a couple of hours doing fatigues, cleaning up, for about an hour and then sent us home. Until, finally, I think they had gathered enough of us to sort of say "We've got a little party of you now, we can send you up to the training depot". Which, for me, was Inglis Barracks at Mill Hill.

* Infantry soldiers of that era refer to "serving with the colours" to indicate regular soldiering, being different from other types of service, such as training or secondments to other units.

** By tradition a shilling, supposedly a gift from a grateful monarch, was given to new recruits to confirm their enlistment. Mythology claimed that having accepted this money the recruit couldn't change their mind about enlisting but, in fact, they could return the shilling and walk away from the Army at any time up until they had sworn the oath of allegiance in front of a magistrate. The origins may go back as far as the Elizabethan era. Shakespeare refers to the King's Penny in Henry VIII, Act III Scene 2. In 1787 a man was hanged for continually accepting the shilling from different recruiting parties and then deserting. He did it 47 times before being caught, but it was quite a common practice on a lesser scale. The awarding of the King's Shilling ceased in 1879, by which time it was the Queen's Shilling, but service personnel still used the colloquialism to refer to enlistment and it was still in use when I joined the RAF in 1968. What my father received was probably half a day's pay plus subsistence allowance. Mythology also has it that tankards were made with glass bottoms so that an innocent couldn't be duped into enlistment by drinking from a tankard into which the King's Shilling had been slipped by a sneaky recruiting Sergeant, but because the shilling could be returned there is no connection with glass bottomed tankards.

# Family Life

My father starts his reminiscences on 10th October 1938, with his enlistment in the British Army. But of course, this wasn't the beginning of the story.

He was born in February 1921, at 10 Shorrolds Road, Fulham. He was the son of Harry George Cubitt, a former Royal Navy rating who had served at the Battle of Jutland (31st May/1st June 1916). According to Dad's birth certificate, Grandad was a general labourer at the time of his birth. He left the Navy in 1919 to help take care of his growing family.

Harry George Cubitt

Dad's mother was Charlotte Eleanor Cubitt, née Jane. Charlotte died of puerperal fever (a uterine infection that was untreatable then) in 1924 shortly after giving birth to her last child, Vera. Vera died in October of the same year at the age of only four months.

This was a tough time for the family. With Charlotte in hospital and five children at home, Grandad Cubitt was unable to hold down a job. How the family survived at all is a bit of a miracle.

Dad was the fourth of the five surviving children, with big brother Harry, elder sisters Lilian and Marjorie and younger sister Edith, known today by one and all as Auntie Edie. Sadly, Auntie Edie died just before this book was published and never got to read of her big brother's exploits. She was the last of her generation of Cubitts. Granddad re-married in 1928 to Emily Davey (née Cake) and a half-brother, Tom, soon followed. With step-sister Queenie and step brother George, it meant eight children living in the house. George died while in his teens, cause unknown.

Charlotte Cubitt (née Jane)

However, the Cubitt's only lived on the upper floor of the house. The lower floor was rented out to the Kelly family, who had thirteen children of their own. The attic room didn't have the dormer window seen in the photo; it was almost certainly a later addition, as some of the other houses in the terrace don't have that feature and they would have been identical when they were built. The flat consisted of a kitchen, bathroom and front bedroom on the first floor of the house. In the attic were two rooms where the children slept, boys at the front and girls at the back. The yard at the rear of the house was part of the downstairs flat and wasn't allowed to be used by the Cubitt family.

Today this part of London is synonymous with fashionable well-heeled Londoners. The leaseholds on houses now change hands for between 600 to 700 thousand pounds or more, but between the two World Wars the area was the home of working class people who earned their livings in the factories and shops in the area and in the riverside industries. Many of the girls went into 'service' ie worked as domestic servants in the houses of the better off. Poverty is a relative thing, but a family living on the wages of an unskilled labourer would not have been well off.

*10 Shorrolds Road as it looks today*

My Auntie Edie recalls the family being "hard-up, but happy". Following the death of Charlotte, the older children were all taken into care and found foster homes. Unfortunately, with George Cubitt having been sacked from work for taking too much time off when his wife and child were ill, the younger two children were also later taken into care. My father was sent to join his older brother Harry in an orphanage near Felixstowe in Suffolk, far too far for his father to visit. The girls were all in foster care on a farm at Gorleston on Sea,

Norfolk. Even after Grandad re-married, the older the three of the five children weren't allowed to return until they reached the age of 16, when they were considered capable of looking after themselves.

My father and Auntie Edie were reunited with their father in October 1928, but Harry Cubitt's erratic employment record prevented the older children from being returned home. The 1930s were a period of great deprivation during and after the Great Depression, with unemployment peaking at 22% in 1933. Harry Cubitt's lack of employment was not untypical.

Dad went to local schools, first Fulham Primary School on nearby Holford Road and then to the secondary school on North End Road. This provided an education aimed at preparing the children to enter into manual labour, domestic service or a much prized apprenticeship; selection was the norm and brighter (or financially better off) children went to Grammar Schools in those days. Normal school leaving age was fourteen and so Dad left school in 1935 to become an apprentice electrician. His enlistment documents from 1938 record him as being an 'Electrician's Mate'.

Although I never knew him as being politically active, Dad must have had some sort of motivation in that direction. Family stories have it that he attended the Battle of Cable Street (4th October 1936) to oppose a march by Sir Oswald Mosely's Blackshirts through a predominantly Jewish neighbourhood.

Family legend has it that he was at Cable Street because he was a member of the Young Communist League, but I have always thought this unlikely given his willingness to join the army in what was, after all, a capitalist country. It is more likely that he was there as a member of his trade union, who were just as opposed to the Blackshirts as the Communists. Certainly, it gives an early indication of Dad's willingness to get involved in a scrap.

In his recording my father said that he was on a very bad road and that was why he joined the army. My Auntie Edie was more direct about this, suggesting that if he hadn't enlisted, he might have ended up in jail. Why this should have come about isn't clear and there isn't anyone around today to ask. I can only assume that he was getting into "bad company", which could mean anything from hanging around on street corners to bank robbery.

These revelations came as a bit of a surprise to me. In all the years I knew him I never knew of a single incident of Dad breaking the law, in which I include not even parking on a double yellow line. He was probably the most honest human being I have ever known. Was it just enlisting in the army that changed him, or was it the fact that it allowed him to escape the poverty of 1930s West London? We shall never know.

Some members of the Cubitt family remained in the Shorrolds Road house right up until Uncle Tom died. He was the youngest of his generation of Cubitts and died in 1990.

But on 10th October 1938 my father joined the army, more specifically The Middlesex Regiment. It's time for Dad to take up his story again.

# 2 – The New Recruit

*Shortly after joining up, 1938*

They (The Middlesex Regiment) were the people who were taking supplementary reserves at the time and they, those people who went in, had a 620 number (my father's full service number was 6203495), which is the same as a Territorial Army number. In other words, it was a Reserve Army number, instead of a 621, which was regular soldier's number.

When I arrived up there (Inglis Barracks), it was a bit of a shock, obviously. Going up there on blind, sort of. Being accepted and pushed in and pushed around. I spent a fortnight up there, mainly engaged in fatigues while the squad for training was being formed up. I went straight into training. Being a machine gun battalion, this consisted of the normal basic training for drill and things like that. Then, after a couple of weeks, we actually started the Vickers Machine Gun training.

[…] You didn't have so much square bashing, because the Vickers Machine Gun itself was a technical animal and there was a lot more training on it. They had just become motorised then and you were trained as a platoon, so a lot of training was getting on trucks, getting off trucks, unloading and mounting the gun and things like that.

Whereas if you had been in the army (infantry) you would be out probably doing field craft and things like that. There was a lot of mechanical training.

We used to go to camp. In those days the army used to go to camp every two years. Most of our training was done in the barracks itself, they had large areas of fields. In places like Gosport there was lots of open space around about at that time.

I feel it was much more interesting training than was normal at that time. […]

I found at the end of my six months there (Inglis Barracks) that I liked the army and I asked for a transfer into the regular army. At that time I had just come up to the age where I could do that. So I signed on then to complete seven years, which was seven years with the colours and five years in the reserves.

From there we were all posted down to Gosport where the 2nd Battalion were at the time. They were feeding (replacements to) the 1st Battalion, who were out in Hong Kong. I stayed down there with them until the outbreak of war.

[…] When war broke we were actually at camp in Savernake Forest and we were wheeled back sharpish to barracks. Then of course it was all hustle and bustle, everybody was sort of getting stores ready and things like that. We were all confined to camp, of course. We were very, very fortunate because, just across the road from the barracks, which had railings all round it, was a very large pub. We used dixies (large cooking vessels with a capacity of about 10 litres), billy cans (smaller cooking vessels, about the size of a standard saucepan) and stuff and get passing civilians to go across the road to the pub to get the beer for us. The NAAFI (Navy, Army and Air Forces Institute – responsible for providing service personnel with leisure facilities) had been closing down because they thought the barracks was going to close. [...]

At the outbreak of war I was still under twenty, and in those days they were not sending people out who were under twenty with the expeditionary force and I was left behind in Gosport. The 2nd/7th Battalion (a Territorial Army unit, mobilised when war broke out) came down and took over in the barracks. From there I was more or less pushed about. I went into the Kensington Regiment (another Territorial unit) for about six months and we were carrying out guard duties at the London Docks.

It was about that time the Small Arms School Corps decided they would set up a demonstration platoon made up of people from the Middlesex Regiment, the Manchester Regiment, the Cheshire Regiment and the Northumberland Fusiliers, which were the four machine gun regiments from the British Army in those days, into a demonstration platoon to do demonstrations for people coming on the courses down at Netheravon.*

[...] The demonstration platoon was used as a training aid, for instance, we would put on a demonstration of a section going into action, or a platoon going into action, or a night firing exercise. They were used to being instructed on what should happen. In other words, it was used as an exhibition as to what should be achieved. And believe me, they did have us trained up to a very, very high standard.

We were very, very disappointed when they did disband us, because although we were four regiments, there was a lot of comradeship. Being the only thing like that we thought we were a little bit special. We always got good reports and things like that. [...]

I had a very good six months down there. It was while we were down there that Dunkirk came about and we were all sort of pushed in to transport to drive down to Bulford station to pick up people coming off the trains that had come in from Dunkirk and, lo and behold, the people I picked up were from my own battalion.

From there, for some reason or another, I can't find out why, I never did find out why, they decided to disband the demonstration platoon (4th September 1940). So obviously I was posted back to the depot at Mill Hill and I was just pushed around from pillar to post up there, moving from place to place to fill in for odd situations. Going out, coming back, they even sent me on a cook's course at one time.

*Dad's certificate of training as a cook, dated 16th April 1941*

Once I got the cook's certificate there was no stopping them. I was sent out attached to people, RE (Royal Engineer) companies, who were being moved near London. There was a shortage of cooks. Then coming back to the holding company again and I was getting very dissatisfied with this as a type of life and I thought to myself "I want to be with a body which is permanent" and it was at that time that they asked for volunteers for special service forces. This didn't actually determine them as parachutists or commandos or whatever. So I volunteered.

At that time, they were training up at Achnacarry, which is the other side of Fort William, and once again, I had a very rude awakening. We got off the train after travelling all night; full marching order, we just took the packs off our backs, threw them into the lorry, then did an eleven mile march into the camp. That was the introduction into the special services.

If you survived the eleven mile march you were selected.

The thing I did like about it, about two miles out they met us with a Scots band, with a pipe band. I've loved pipe music ever since.


\* The Machinegun Training Centre (MTC) at Netheravon had been taken over by the Small Arms School Corps in 1926.

# The Early Days of the Commandos

My father has taken us up to August 1941, but the Commandos had already been in existence for over a year by then.

Following the evacuation from Dunkirk in June 1940, Winston Churchill realised that a significant factor in eventually defeating Nazi Germany would be the morale of the British people. The German Army was on the other side of the English Channel, preparing to invade Britain and the victory of the RAF in the Battle of Britain couldn't be predicted. The country faced a dangerous and uncertain future.

The willingness of the people to continue to fight the war over a period of several years would test the country to the limit. To maintain morale the British people had to believe they could win. Churchill therefore devised a plan that he hoped would help to bolster morale. If he could drip feed news of small victories to the people, he might convince them that ultimate victory wasn't just feasible, it was inevitable. At the same time, Britain could continually chip away at the morale of the enemy by constantly harrying them.

Remembering the hit and run tactics of the Boers in South Africa, where he had served in the army and also been a War Correspondent for The Morning Post, Churchill understood how detrimental to morale such attacks could be. It provided him with a model for how to harass the enemy, damaging their morale while maintaining that of the British people.

In June 1940 Churchill called for a force to be assembled and equipped to inflict casualties on the Germans and bolster British morale. He told the joint Chiefs of Staff to submit proposals for offensives against German occupied Europe and described the need for men of 'the hunter class' to 'develop a reign of terror along the enemy coast'.

Earlier in the war the Army had recruited Independent Companies for guerrilla operations in Norway. These hadn't come about, mainly because there was no way to keep such a force re-supplied, but they provided an early pool of volunteers for the first commandos and provide a building block for them. The first commando raid, Operation Collar, took place on 23rd June 1940. This was carried out by No 11 Independent Company and the raid was on an area of the French coast between Boulogne-Sur-Mer and Le Touquet, though it was very small scale and inflicted no significant damage.

No 1 Commando formed on 13th June 1940 with men from Nos 6 and 8 Independent companies. They then became No 1 Special Service Battalion before returning to their original title of No 1

Commando again in 1941, taking some troops from No 1 Special Service Battalion with the remainder going to No 2 Commando.

No 2 Commando formed on 22$^{nd}$ June 1940 and were intended to become the parachute arm of the commandos. Consequently, they didn't operate as a Commando while they concentrated on their parachute training. In November 1940 they were re-designated as 11 Special Air Service Battalion (no connection to the modern SAS which was founded in 1942 by David Stirling) and in September 1941 they would be renamed again, this time becoming the 1$^{st}$ Battalion the Parachute Regiment, the name they hold today. No 2 Commando was re-established on 26$^{th}$ February 1941.

So it was that Captain John Durnford-Slater of the Royal Artillery volunteered for service with the Commandos, was promoted to the rank of Lieutenant Colonel on 23$^{rd}$ June 1940 and ordered to raise No 3 Commando. In fact Durnford-Slater was the whole Commando, as he had no officers or men until he recruited them. Like No1 Commando, they were renamed No 3 Special Service Battalion, but Durnford-Slater hated the title because of the initials and refused to use it, thereby creating something of a stand-off. The War Office would address correspondence to him as Commanding Officer, No 3 Special Service Battalion and he would reply signing off as Commanding Officer, No 3 Commando. In the end the War Office blinked first and the Special Service designation was quietly dropped in favour of 'Commando'.

He was told to recruit from Southern Area Command, from units stationed along the South Coast, from Southampton to Cornwall and north into Somerset. He quickly set about interviewing officer candidates who had also responded to the call for volunteers. In the process he recruited the man who would one day replace him, a young Lieutenant by the name of Peter Young of the Bedfordshire & Hertfordshire Regiment.

He recruited one Captain and two Lieutenants for each of the ten troops of the commando, then sent them out to recruit the soldiers they would command, based on the criteria that had been set down. These included 'men of good physique', 'initiative and leadership', 'able to swim and navigate boats' and a willingness to undertake 'hazardous work'.

Despite the speed of the recruitment process the volunteers were, by and large, of good quality. Many were veterans of Dunkirk, wishing to retaliate against the Germans. Others, like my father, were hoping to escape the tedium of garrison life.

Regardless of their substantive rank these first volunteers all joined the Commando with the rank of Private and had to earn their promotions all over again, based on the commando criteria and their ability to act on their own initiative in particular.

The commando formed at Plymouth and started to train for their first operation. On the night of 14th/15th July 1940, 3 Commando carried out its first raid, Operation Ambassador.

There is a saying amongst pilots who have survived a crash landing, that any landing that you can walk away from is a good landing*. If you view Operation Ambassador in that light, it was a good operation. However, it was more generally recognised as being something of a shambles (not my words).

The concept of operations for the raid were simple enough. No 11 Independent Company would land on one side of the occupied island of Guernsey and attack the airfield, blowing up any aircraft they found and generally causing mayhem. At the same time men from H Troop, 3 Commando, would land on the south side of the island to distract the four hundred and sixty nine strong German garrison. The force was to be transported across the channel in two Royal Navy destroyers, HMS Scimitar and HMS Saladin, before transferring to six RAF air-sea rescue launches to be ferried ashore.

Unfortunately, due to an error in degaussing (getting rid of unwanted magnetic fields that might affect the boats' compasses) the compasses of the launches were pointing South when they should have been pointing North.

11 Independent Company's boats headed in the wrong direction. Two had to drop out with engine trouble and the other ended up on Sark, where the troops hunted in vain for an airfield. It could have

been worse, if they had kept going they could have landed in occupied France.

However, H Troop fared better. One of the RAF personnel on the launch realised the cliffs that should have been in front of them were behind them and reversed course, with the other launches in the small flotilla following, and so the troop made it ashore at the planned location.

The launches weren't designed for this work, so couldn't get close to the beach and when the soldiers clambered over the side they found themselves up to their chests in water. The raid had been delayed by 24 hours so the tides weren't as anticipated and instead of sand beneath their feet they had to contend with slippery boulders as they waded ashore.

After hours of stumbling about in the dark the troop failed to make contact with any of the enemy garrison. They cut the cables to the telegraph hut that connected the island to France, but in the end Durnford-Slater ordered his troops back to the beach without them firing a shot.

Unfortunately the tide was now at full ebb, forcing the launches to withdraw from the beach into deeper water. The commandos had to swim for it.

They loaded their weapons into a rubber dingy which was pulled back to the launches on the end of a rope. Sadly the man on board the dingy, looking after the weapons, fell overboard. Then Durnford-Slater was approached by three rather shame-faced soldiers who confessed to not being able to swim. Dawn was approaching, so time didn't allow for the rubber dingy to be sent back for them. There was no alternative but to leave them behind.

The missing man from the dingy later joined the three non-swimmers and between them they evaded capture for two days, but they were eventually taken prisoner and managed to persuade the Germans that they were merely stragglers from the British Expeditionary Force in France who had tried to escape via Guernsey. They spent the rest of the war in a Prisoner of War camp.

Churchill was not amused by the raid's failure and ordered that troops shouldn't be frittered away on such flea bites in the future. Durnford-Slater, in the meantime, studied the lessons of the raid and used it to improve the training of his men, especially in relation to boat handling, navigation and swimming.

In September 1940 the Commando relocated to Inveraray, one of the locations where Commando training was to be concentrated until Achnacarry House took on the role. It was here that the commandos first encountered properly constructed landing craft.

*On Exercise, Scotland, a troop of commandos preparing to disembark from a landing craft.*

The next operation was everything that the first had failed to be. Operation Claymore was launched on 4th March 1941 against the Lofoten Islands.

The Lofotens are a group of islands off the north west coast of Norway, about eight hundred and fifty miles from Scapa Flow (Orkney Islands) and well inside the Arctic Circle. They had been occupied by the Germans as part of their conquest of Norway.

The objectives of the mission were fairly simple. The Lofoten Islands were major producers of fish oil, needed by the Germans for the manufacture of certain types of explosives. The primary objective was therefore to destroy the fish oil factories. In addition, the commandos were to capture German prisoners, arrest Quislings** and to bring back any Norwegians who wanted to volunteer to serve with the Free Norwegian Navy.

Nos 3 and 4 Commando were tasked with mounting the operation and 3 Commando was allocated HMS Princess Beatrix as their primary form of transport. It was a former Belgian cross channel steamer and along with its sister ships, HMS Prince Leopold, HMS Prince Charles and HMS Queen Emma (Dutch), was well suited for its task. These were ships that the commandos would come to know well over the next three years. Norwegians under the command of Martin Linge *** would act as guides and interpreters.

The Commando was broken down into smaller groups, each with a different destination once they had landed. The landings came as a complete surprise to the Germans and were unopposed. When he got to the local post office Lieutenant R L J Willis sent a very cheeky telegram addressed to Adolf Hitler, referring him to a recent speech he had made that predicted that German troops would meet the English wherever they landed, and asked where the German troops were.

In all, the operation destroyed eighteen factories, sunk twenty thousand tons of shipping in the harbours, destroyed significant stocks of fuel and captured two hundred and nineteen German prisoners and sixty quislings (some accounts say it was two hundred and twenty eight prisoners, I have used Durnford-Slater's figure). A considerable amount of intelligence materials were also seized. One hundred and fifty Norwegian volunteers were taken off with the troops when they withdrew. There were no casualties amongst the raiding force.

As 3 Commando's landing craft departed, the Norwegians crammed the quayside, cheering the commandos and singing the Norwegian National Anthem.

The Commando moved to Largs shortly after the Lofoten Islands raid. Later that year Lt Col Durnford-Smith heard that there were some useful men being trained at the Commando Replacement Depot at Achnacarry and went up to see if he could recruit any of them to fill gaps in his ranks created by soldiers who had been returned to unit or who had been transferred to other commandos preparing to leave for North Africa.

On arrival Durnford-Slater met one of the instructors, who had previously served with 3 Commando. Hearing that his colleague and rival, Dudley Lister of 4 Commando, was about to arrive on a similar mission, he arranged for the soldiers he had his eye on to dress in their shabbiest uniforms and to carry out a training scheme and not do it very well. Meanwhile, the candidates he wasn't interested in were to parade in best battledress and carry out some smart drill movements. Needless to say, Dudley Lester selected the well-dressed soldiers and Durnford-Slater got the pick of the litter, so to speak.

And that was how, on 26th August 1941, the story of 3 Commando and my father's story started to become one and the same.

I think my father was being a little bit economical with the truth when he gives his reason for leaving the Machine Gun Demonstration Platoon in 1940. His military records show him having just completed twenty eight days in a military detention centre and being posted back to his battalion on the day of his release. What offence he committed to get him sent there isn't stated, but my mother once mentioned that my father had punched an officer for suggesting that his uniform wasn't up to standard on parade; twenty eight days would have been about the correct sentence for an offence such as that and the posting back to his battalion from would have been an additional measure to separate him from the officer he assaulted.

My father may have miss-remembered the distance between Fort William and Achnacarry, because it is actually seventeen miles. But the march was the traditional greeting for new arrivals at the training centre.

* Attributed to American Air Force test pilot Chuck Yeager, the first pilot to fly faster than the speed of sound. The rest of the quote goes "and if you can fly the plane the next day it's an outstanding landing".

** Norwegians who sided with the Germans, named after the Norwegian puppet Prime Minister Vidkun Qisling.

*** Martin Linge was the Commanding Officer of Norwegian Independent Company 1 and became renowned for his service to his country, taking part in several operations until he was killed in action at Màløy (see chapter 5). After his death The Norwegian Independent Company 1 became known informally as Linge Company.

# 3 – Achnacarry

There were about half a dozen of us who went up from Mill Hill (Inglis Barracks). There was a full Corporal, who managed to disappear when we got to Euston and get himself a sleeper berth. We didn't see him again until the following morning when we got off.

There was a big intake from all the other volunteers that had arrived there, at the same time, from all the other regiments. The idea of the Special Services, in those days, was that you did three months up there, doing the training that they wanted you to do. Then you were to go down to Ringway (now Manchester Airport) where you started parachute training.

[…] We lived in Nissen huts, they had put Nissen huts up on concrete hard-standings. We used to actually live in those, we used to go out, get wet through, come back in, whip our cloths off and put them in the drying room and go back the following morning to get them back again. I swear that that whoever was in charge up there turned the dryers off because I don't think I ever got into dry cloths in the morning.

We did route marches, speed marches, individual orientation marches and things like that. They had an assault course up there which has never been known to be done by one man alone. Of course, this started off the actual basic training of the commandos, what they used to call 'me and my pal', where you always worked in pairs, wherever you went. It was a very, very good idea.

The assault course was a very stiff one. It was right up the side of a mountain, over trees and bogs and swing ropes and what not.

We also used to do opposed landings, up there. The boats we used up there were the Goatley boats, the ones used with a paddle. They took a full section of men and we used to go in on opposed landings there with instructors throwing stun grenades, plus Bren guns were firing on fixed lines and things like that. It was all good experience.

I left my Vickers machinegun behind. I didn't actually go back to the Vickers until I went back to the battalion after I'd been through my commando service.

If you fell out on a speed march or a long route march you were automatically returned back to your unit (known as RTU, it was also the punishment for poor discipline). There was no question about it. If you couldn't do it, you just weren't good enough. You weren't given any second chance at all, there was no appeal or anything like that. Your kit was packed and you went back to your unit.

I should say, probably, about ten percent of every intake that went up there were RTU'd. A lot got through though.

It's rumoured that they had an allowance up there (for training casualties), and because of the type of training they were allowed more casualties. They were always expecting some casualties on training.

The PT (physical training) was done with tree logs. It was the first time I'd seen the bottom of a pine tree. There used to be six men on a tree trunk. You threw it over your head, forwards and passed it back and the back man ran round the front. It built you up to a good standard of physical fitness. And, of course, we had unarmed combat, we were taught by two ex-Shanghai policemen. They used to teach the drill with fighting knives. […]

But at that time the commandos were already in existence and half way through our course the CO (Commanding Officer) of No 3 Commando (Lt Col Durnford-Slater), who had just come back from Lofoten, came up looking for recruits. No 8 Commando had just been split off from them and had taken a lot of the personnel and they went out to the Middle East with Layforce (a brigade sized force of commandos formed under Col Robert Laycock).

Having had a very, very wet time up there, there was quite a few of us who volunteered to go on his selection board. He came through and selected us, came and watched us working and things like that and selected the people he wanted.

From there, we didn't actually complete the full course, because he had a need for men and we went down and were posted to Largs, on the Ayrshire Coast, just along from Glasgow, where most of the commandos at that time were being trained, around Inveraray, the Scottish lochs, the Kyle of Bute.

# A Short History of Achnacarry.

Achnacarry House is in the Lochaber region of the Scottish Highlands, sitting on a neck of land between Loch Lochy and Loch Arkaig. It is the ancestral home of Clan Cameron. The original house was built in 1655 but the more modern structure, seen today, was built in 1802.

At the outbreak of World War II the Cameron Clan made the house and grounds available to the War Office, but with the war effort being focused on France there was little use for the estate until the commandos started training in Scotland. With the decision to focus commando training on Inveraray and Lochailort, the house provided a suitable location at which to base volunteers until they could be called forward for training. It was named the Commando Depot, though Brigadier Durnford-Slater refers to it as the Commando Replacement Depot. Later, it was decided to concentrate training in a single location and Achnacarry was selected to become the Commando Basic Training Centre, with its first courses starting in March 1942.

As well as training British Commandos, it also trained soldiers from the 'Free' forces of the occupied nations of Europe, who formed 10 (Inter-Allied) Commando. When America entered the war, they wanted to form their own equivalent to the commandos, calling them Rangers and they, too, did their training at Achnacarry. In all some 25,000 commandos passed through the depot and the training centre.

The troops were allocated to one of three training 'houses': Keyes, Haydon or Sturges, named after the founders of combined operations. Within each 'house' were four training troops commanded by an officer, who was also a trainee, and aided by an

NCO instructor. In addition, there was a demonstration troop which also provided the pipe band.

Much of the training focused on toughening the men up so that they would be able undertake their future roll. In addition, they were taught the combat skills that they would need, as well as specialist skills such as orienteering, boat handling, water borne assaults, demolition and rock climbing.

Quite a lot of the training involved the use of live ammunition and quite a lot of it took place at night. As a consequence of that there were sixteen commando deaths in training at Achnacarry and more deaths amongst the American Rangers.

*Crossing a toggle rope\* bridge during training.*

The centre closed in 1946 and the estate was handed back to the Clan Cameron. In 1952, Her Majesty Queen Elizabeth, the Queen Mother (wife of George VI), dedicated a memorial to the Commandos that stands beside the A82 road out of Spean Bridge, heading towards Fort Augustus. You can't miss it, it's 17 ft (5.8 metres) high. Next to it is a small area for the remembrance of the Commandos who passed through Achnacarry. My family placed a plaque there when we scattered my father's ashes in 2011.

*November Sun at the Memorial*

If you ever pass by, please spare a moment to stand at that memorial and remember those who made the ultimate sacrifice for their country. You might also be interested in visiting the Commando Museum, a private collection of commando memorabilia that is housed at the Spean Bridge Hotel.

The inclusion of unarmed combat and knife fighting in the training are of particular note. The two former Shanghai police officers that my father referred to were Eric Anthony Sykes and William Ewart Fairbairn. They had been commissioned into the

British Army in 1940 with their specific skill sets in mind, as both were too old for normal enlistment into the army (Fairbairn was 45 and Sykes was 43). As well as training commandos and Rangers, they also trained agents of the Special Operations Executive (SOE) who would parachute into occupied Europe to carry out spying missions or to work with local resistance groups.

Sykes and Fairbairn made no bones about the nature of the training they provided. There were none of the gentlemen's rules that would be found in the boxing ring or the dojo. The objective was plain and simple: get your opponent on the ground by any means available and make sure they don't get up again.

Lieutenant P A Porteus of 4 Commando had particular reason to remember these lessons. Participating in Operation Cauldron, part of the 1942 Dieppe raid, he was shot at close range through the hand, by a German soldier. He grappled with him, took the German's own bayonet from him and killed him with it.

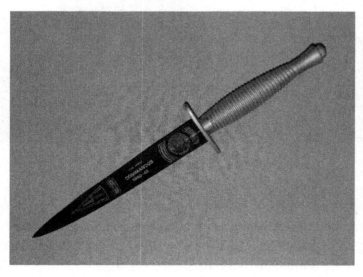

*The Fairbairn-Sykes Fighting Knife. This is a souvenir replica. The original would have had a black handle.*

As well as providing training Sykes and Fairbairn also designed the most famous weapon that was to become associated with the commandos, the Fairbairn-Sykes fighting knife, also known as the Commando dagger. It became the symbol of the commandos and remains so today. The first batch of knives were produced by Wilkinson Sword Ltd in January 1941.

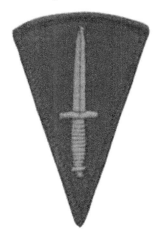

*The Symbol of the Commandos*

The march from Fort William to Achnacarry was unnecessary in terms of transportation. There is a much closer railway station in the nearby village of Spean Bridge, on the line from Fort William to Inverness. However, the march was a quick way of separating the no-hopers from the real possibilities amongst the volunteers. Those that survived the march, either through physical fitness or sheer bloody mindedness, were then subjected to more selection tests and interviews to establish their suitability.

A later addition to the psychological testing of the volunteers was a line of crosses on the approach to the camp, supposedly marking the graves of those of volunteers who had died during training. They were, in fact, fakes. Donald Gilchrist, author of Castle Commando, recalls reading a couple of the inscriptions on the crosses. They said things like "He showed himself on the skyline" and "He failed to take cover on an assault landing".

The soldiers lived in Nissen huts while officers lived in the main house. For the soldiers the water for washing was invariably cold, the food filling but unimaginative.

A typical first day of training would be to take a truck to Fort William, climb 1,345 metres (approximately 4,371 ft) up Ben Nevis (regardless of the weather) and then march eighteen miles back to Achnacarry.

Officers didn't have a batman (personal servant) to clean their kit. If the men had to clean their own kit then the officers had to do the same, otherwise how could they know if the men had enough time to do it? This would have been quite a culture shock to some of the officers who were used to a more pampered life.

A regular feature of the training was the 'speed march', which was done while wearing full combat equipment and carrying a rifle and ammunition. These were a progress test for the soldiers, carried out against the clock. At the end of the first week it was a not too challenging 5 miles in 60 minutes.

A pace of one mile in ten minutes was the benchmark for all future marches. A seven-mile march was concluded with the troops having to dig a defensive position. The nine-mile march was followed by firing practice, the twelve-mile march by a drill parade and the final, seventeen mile, march was concluded with a session on the assault course and firing practice. The times, however, were only guides. Troop commanders were expected to aim for faster times for their troop. Teamwork was essential, with the fitter members of the troop helping the stragglers and loads being shared around. The clock didn't stop until the last man of the troop crossed the finish line. I'm surprised that my father's estimate of a ten percent attrition rate was so low and it speaks well for the motivation of the volunteers and for the quality of the training that was provided.

My father's recollections match well with those of Donald Gilchrist. It was hard work, but no one ever had time to be bored. If you weren't training, you were probably sleeping or cleaning your kit.

The green beret which, like the Fairbairn-Sykes fighting knife, became synonymous with the Commandos wasn't introduced until 1942.

It was the CO of 1 Commando that first put forward the idea of a distinctive headdress for the commandos. As the soldiers were drawn from all the different regiments of the British Army they all wore different styles of headdress, from the Glengarry's and Tam o'shanters of the Scottish regiments, the Caubeens of the Irish, through the various styles of forage caps and berets of the English regiments. He thought it would aid esprit d'corps, a sense of belonging, if all his soldiers wore the same type of hat.

It was pointed out that the Royal Tank Regiment were allowed to wear a black beret, and in July of 1942 the Parachute Regiment had been authorised to wear a maroon beret, so why not a beret of a specific colour for the commandos? Eventually the War Office agreed and on 13th October 1942 an order was sent out authorising the issue of green berets to the commandos. The first issue was made to 1 Commando, partly because it was their suggestion and partly because they were just about to depart to take part in the Operation Torch landings in North Africa. The soldiers still, however, wore their own regimental cap badges.

The green beret is still worn by the Royal Marine Commandos and specialist army units attached to them.

The dates on my father's Army record (Army Form B103-2) for this period are somewhat confusing and conflict with his account. He recalls completing about half of a 3 month training course at Achnacarry, but his records show him as being there for only a few days. On 15th August 1940 he is shown as being posted, but with no destination. On 21st August he is shown as being posted again, this time to the Special Training Battalion Holding Wing, which was at Achnacarry and on the 26th August he is shown as being posted to 3 Commando. The relevant three entries all carry the same initials and may, therefore, have been entered retrospectively and inaccurately.

The previous entry was made on 22nd June and showed him ceasing to be attached to one of the units he'd been sent to as a cook

(207 Company, Pioneer Corps), so I suspect that he may have departed for Achnacarry earlier than his record shows, perhaps early in July, which would account for the discrepancy between my father's records and his own recollections. However, we can assume that on 26th August 1941 my father moved to Largs to join 3 Commando.

* A six foot long rope with a loop at one end and a wooden toggle, like those found on duffle coats, on the other so they could be joined together. All the commandos carried one, wrapped around their waists. At Achnacarry, one of the exercises was to build a bridge made entirely from toggle ropes, but I don't think one was ever used in combat.

# 4 – Largs

We went down there to join No 3 Commando and things were very much easier down there. We were put in civilian billets for which we got the princely sum of seven (shillings) and six (pence) a day subsistence allowance (about thirty-eight pence (£0.38)), which was supposed to be paid to the landlady, but none of the landladies took more than about half of that off us for food.

I had a year there with them, actually, in Largs. Just after we arrived there, we started training for the Vågsøy raid. Things got a bit hectic then and we spent the best part of our time up in Inveraray, getting on boats, getting off boats, and doing boat drill and things like that and doing assaults.

Their favourite one was to run us off the boat and up to Cash (Dun na Cuaiche) monument, which was a great big monument (actually a watch tower) on top of a dirty big hill just outside Inveraray Castle. Then we when we got back, we had to swim back to the boats. There were no half measures with them at all.

[…] You were putting it all (the training) into practice. The pressure when you got to a commando wasn't quite so much. You were already part of an organisation that was already doing it, so there wasn't an awful lot of pressure on it.

Plus, too, discipline was a little bit more lax. You were given a bit more leeway to think for yourself and do things for yourself without disobeying an order. You were taught individual self-reliance. But, if you stepped out of line, you were pushed off. There was no doubt about it. This happened throughout all the commandos. The greatest fear of any commando was to be returned to his unit. It was a great stigma. It used to keep them well in line. You used to have one or two of them, obviously. You could never get one hundred percent good boys, do you? We used to do quite well on the discipline side and it was that little bit more relaxed than a normal battalion would be.

There was one incident. The RSM was out of one of the cavalry regiments and to see him take infantry men on a drill parade was really marvellous. Some of the orders we used to get were great. But we used to get through it and he did his job and he did it well. Unfortunately, he got taken prisoner and was killed two days after he was released from the prison camp. He fell off a tank he was riding on. Poor man.

We had leave, a normal amount of leave. But every time we went out, when we came back from Vågsøy we got leave. Every time we did a raid, we got a couple of weeks leave afterwards, which was a bit extra to what we normally got.

Largs was a seaside town for Glasgow and we never had to worry about entertainment. At the weekend and whenever we were free there were always girls coming down from Glasgow and there were two cinemas there and a dance hall. We were quite well off. It was still acting very much as a seaside town. Very much as Southend is to London. We were very well catered for.

Our 2I/C (second in command) at that time was Major Churchill, Jack Churchill. He had the reputation for being a bit mad, his nickname was actually Mad Jack. He used to walk around with a claymore in his hand and he went ashore at Lofoten actually playing the bagpipes himself. *

He was a great character, actually, but a stickler for work. He really got us down to it up there.


* The incident with the bag pipes was actually at Maaloy, not the Lofoten islands and is well documented. He also repeated it on later raids. But he is also credited of killing a German with a longbow in May 1940, the only known British soldier to do such a thing since the longbow was replaced by the musket. Playing his bagpipes (it is suggested that the tune was Will Ye No Come Back Again) during a raid in Yugoslavia with 40 Commando, he was knocked unconscious and captured. He spent the rest of the war in Sachsenhausen Concentration Camp until he was evacuated to the Tyrol by the SS, along with 120 other prominent prisoners. It must be assumed that he

would have been executed under the Fuhrer Order (see Appendix B) but a German army unit forced the SS to hand over the prisoners, almost certainly saving their lives.

# Life on the Clyde

There is little that can be added to my father's account of life while he was at Largs. The commandos were kept busy training in the hills or on the lochs behind the town or at locations such as Inveraray. No one knew when the Commando would be called on to mount their next operation, but all knew that it could be at short notice and so the commandos had to maintain peak efficiency at all times. Many operations were planned, but they were each cancelled in turn for being too risky or as military priorities shifted.

My father recalls that discipline was reasonably relaxed, but Durnford-Slater recalls differently.

As the Commando lived within the local community, Durnford-Slater knew that he was heavily reliant on the good will of the local population. He therefore couldn't allow poor discipline to impact on that. He believed that he ran a tight ship and breaches of discipline were immediately punished with the dreaded RTU. This is probably a matter of perception. My father had been no stranger to the CO's Orderly Room* before joining the commandos, so he may have felt that discipline was more relaxed while they were in Largs.

Discipline in the Commando was maintained the Regimental Police (RPs - drawn from within the commandos and nothing to do with the Military Police) led by two notable characters, Sgt Bill Chitty, a former heavy weight boxer and policeman, and Sgt Lofty King, aided by a few other tough types. They ruled with a rod of iron and weren't slow to use their fists if shouting and threats didn't work. This kept most of the commandos in line and out of the CO's view. The local police occasionally called on the (unofficial) assistance of the RPs when gangs of itinerant labourers working in the area started to get unruly.

As described by my father, the soldiers lived in billets in the local community, handing over their subsistence allowance to pay for their food, heating, laundry etc. Close bonds were forged between the soldiers and their hosts and the local community came to regard the commando as 'their' soldiers.

It was here that 3 Commando started to get involved in rock climbing. Two officers were keen on rock climbing, Lieutenant Algy Forrester and an Australian by the name of Lieutenant Bill Lloyd. Forrester was the expert and trained Lloyd in the necessary skills. It was their idea to start landing in the less obvious places, such as beaches where the enemy might be waiting, instead landing on rocky shores and below cliffs where they could maintain the element of surprise. They worked out a technique where one man would climb a cliff and anchor a rope at the top so that others could pull themselves up. A drawing of a commando doing that was used on the front of the original paperback version for John Durnford-Slater's book.

3 Commando became specialists in this type of assault and practiced it until they became experts. It was a skill that was to cost them dear later in the war. In due course a specialist rock climbing school was established at Glen Coe to train instructors who would, in turn, train their units.

My father must have learnt to rock climb, along with the rest of 3 Commando, but I never heard of him doing it after the war. I therefore suspect it wasn't one of the things he enjoyed doing.

* Commanding Officer's Orderly Room. A sort of military Magistrate's Court where the Commanding Officer administers justice in accordance with King's Regulations and the Manual of Military Law (or their modern equivalents). Offences range from the trivial, such as being late on parade, to the more serious such as being absent without leave (AWOL) or disobeying an order. Powers of punishment range from admonishments and small fines through to detention for up to 30 days. More serious offences are dealt with by Court Marshall. Durnford-Slater, like most Commando COs, didn't

bother with Orderly Rooms. If a soldier didn't behave, he was on the next train back to his unit, with no second chance.

# 5 – Vågsøy/Måløy

[...] It was Christmas '41 we were actually supposed to do the raid. It was supposed to happen on Christmas Day, but the passage over was so stormy that the landing craft ships had to stop. We had to put into Shetland to pump out, so the raid didn't take place on Christmas morning, it took place on Boxing Day morning. [...]

We were told nothing. We were told that we were going to train for raiding purposes, then about a week before, no, a fortnight before, they withdrew us from Largs, put us on landing ships and took us up to Inverarry and kept us on the landing ships and that was when our briefings started.

We didn't know where it was, we were going to until it was two days before, on the way we went up to the Orkneys and actually did a couple of practice raids up there on the islands.

We went in what were then called landing ships, infantry landing ships. Before the war they were cross channel steamers. Two Belgian ones, the Leopold and the Charles and two Dutch, the Beatrix and the Emma. Instead of having lifeboats on the ships they had assault landing craft.

The way you got on the landing craft, they used to drop the davits down to deck level, you actually loaded in. Then you went down a certain way, strung out along the side of the boats, until they decided to drop you. They used to drop you down as you were still on the move and the Cox'n used to take up the way as you went along. It was very, very cleverly done. They used to do it without stopping. The idea was not to make the boat a stationary target.

Actually going into the hot zone, I found that I'd never had such an eerie sensation. After being loaded into the boats we held up at deck level, for somewhere about a quarter of an hour and we were steaming up the fjord, big white cliffs on either side. It was so quiet, all you could hear was the wake of the stern wave as the boat was going along. It was a very eerie feeling. It was my first time going into action, which made it all the worse. So it was quite an experience.

Unfortunately, when we came into the landing craft and started away, we were hit by a smoke bomb; the Beaufighters were dropping smoke. One of them got hit by German ack-ack fire, or something, he dropped a smoke bomb right in the middle of our section in the landing craft and only about half a dozen of us got out. Everyone else was very badly phosphorus burnt.

Fortunately, I was in the back, tail-end Charlie of the section and I managed to hop over the side and I got away with very, very few burns. I got a little bit on my wrist and a scar on the side of the face.

I swam ashore, it was very cold. I had a two pound pack of explosive on my back, which worried me immensely. It was the first thing I took off and threw back into the water, because knowing it was phosphorus on it, it would break out once again when it got dry. Our medical section set up a post and I was sent back to the ship. That was all I saw of the Vågsøy raid, though it was one of the very, very hard-fought raids.

We were all carrying explosives, as our troop were acting as demolition troop at that time. We were to go along, blowing up the fish oil factories, as and when we were called forward to do the work. It was mainly gun cotton slabs and primers in those days.

You had your normal weapons, some of the section commanders had Tommy Guns, the rest had rifles and you had a Bren gun section of course.

I was seen by an MO (Medical Officer – more likely actually an orderly), put in a boat and sent back. By the time I got back to the ship they had made the Wardroom (officers' dining area) into a casualty clearing station on board ship. I laid there and on the way back we were met by a hospital ship and we were taken back to Aberdeen and spent three weeks in Aberdeen hospital.

I was a lucky man. It was my first time in action and we lost quite a lot of people on that raid. I've always believed that I was one of God's chosen, because I went through the war with only those little scratches I've mentioned.

So the Vågsøy (Known as Vaagso by the English) raid was very little in the way of myself. After I came out of hospital, I came out of hospital on my twenty-first birthday actually.* I was sent away on three weeks recuperation leave which I spent down in London, then went back.

Then after we went back we went back to normal training. Running over the hills and such. We went back to Largs again.

* For the dates to correspond with both my father's recollections and his military record, he must has spent some time in a convalescent home as well as the three weeks in hospital.

# Operation Archery

Operation Archery (27th December 1941, not 26th December as my father remembers), as the raid on Vågsøy/Måløy was to be designated, was the third in a series of raids on the Norwegian coast. The Lofoton Islands raid, discussed in Chapter 2, was the first and on 11th December 1941 a sizeable force from 6 and 9 commandos (Operation Kitbag) set off to attack the town of Floss, but the Naval commander of the raid was unsure of his location prior to the landing and the raid had to be aborted. Although cancelled, the raid still incurred casualties. While the commandos were priming grenades below deck, one went off, killing six men and wounding another eleven.

This operation was much further south than the earlier ones, a small town in a fjord situated between Bergen to the south and Trondheim to the north. The area benefited from air cover from the Luftwaffe and was better defended on the ground, including artillery batteries sited on Måløy island (spelled as Maaloy by the British and the spelling I will use), covering the strait through which the taskforce would have to approach. A diversionary raid, Operation Anklet, would be carried out on the Lofoten Islands once again.

The town of South Vågsøy (known as Vaagso to the British) was home to several fish oil refineries, which were the primary target, just as they had been for Operation Claymore. Secondary objectives were, once again, the subduing of the garrison and capture of prisoners, the arrest of Quislings and the recruitment of volunteers to join the Free Norwegian forces.

No 3 Commando provided the majority of the force, with two troops from 2 Commando, a medical section from 4 Commando and a party of Royal Engineers from 6 Commando who were demolition experts. A detachment from Norwegian Independent Company 1, under Martin Linge, would again provide guides and interpreters. With the Royal Navy providing transport and warships and the Royal Air Force providing air cover, this truly was to be a 'combined operation' as envisaged by the War Office.

*The Combined Operations shoulder patch.*

The total number of soldiers involved came to fifty one officers and five hundred and twenty five other ranks.

The Royal Navy representation was one cruiser, HMS Kenya, and four destroyers: HMS Onslow, HMS Oribi, HMS Offa and HMS Chiddingfield, plus the landing ships Prince Leopold and Prince Charles. The submarine HMS Tuna was to provide a navigational marker to guide the ships into the approach channel for the fjord.

The RAF committed a force of Hampden Bombers and Beaufighters, while a force of Blenheims from 114 Squadron was to cause a distraction by bombing the nearby airfield at Herdla.

The commandos were divided into four forces. The first was to attack the hamlet of Holevik, the second group landed just to the south of the town of South Vaagso while the third group landed on Maaloy. The fourth group were a floating reserve, to be deployed as needed by the commander of the land forces, Lt Col Durnford-Slater.

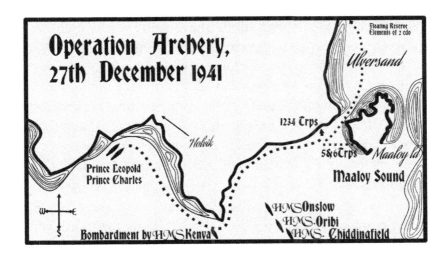

The overall operation was a success. In the initial bombardment by HMS Kenya three of the four guns of the artillery battery on Maaloy were knocked out and the barrage was only lifted when the attacking commandos went ashore. They made very short work of the remaining gun and the defending German gunners and the fighting was over in twenty minutes. The attacking force then crossed the water to join the attack on South Vaagso.

As recalled by my father later in his account, the Maaloy assault force was led ashore by Major 'Mad Jack' Churchill playing the bag pipes. According to Saunders' (see Bibliography) account of the landing he was playing "The March of the Cameron Men".

The eight defenders who were supposed to be at Holevik turned out to be enjoying breakfast in South Vaagso, so the attackers there had very little to do and soon moved on to join the groups attacking the town.

The attack on South Vaagso itself was more demanding. Unknown to anyone, a detachment of fifty elite German troops were enjoying a Christmas vacation in the town and assisted in its defence. However, the commando ethos of always moving forward and maintaining the impetus of the attack made sure that all the objectives were met, though there were casualties.

For a full account of the operation I would recommend Joseph H Devin's book, details of which can be found in the bibliography.

In all, four fish oil factories were destroyed, nine merchant ships totalling fifteen thousand tons were sunk, one hundred and fifty Germans were killed, ninety eight captured and seventy one volunteers from the Norwegian population went to the UK with the returning forces.

The attacking force began their withdrawal at about two in the afternoon, which would have been about dusk that far north at that time of year. They returned to Scapa Flow without further incident.

On the negative side, two British Officers and fifteen other ranks (ORs) were killed, along with the Norwegian, Martin Linge. Five British officers and forty eight ORs were wounded, along with two Norwegian ORs. The Royal Navy suffered minor damage to HMS Kenya and two naval ratings were killed and two officers and four ratings wounded. But it was the RAF who suffered the most losses. Two Hampdens, seven Blenheims and two Beaufighters were shot down, with all of their thirty one aircrew killed.

As for the measure of the commando's immediate success, they captured more German prisoners in the Claymore and Archery operations than had been taken during the entire period between the declaration of war and the evacuation of Dunkirk ten months later.

However, it was in the aftermath of the raid that the most significant damage was done to the German war effort. Hitler became convinced that the repeated attacks on Norway signalled an intent by Britain to mount a full-scale invasion, possibly as a prelude to an invasion of Denmark to open the way for an invasion of Germany itself. Consequently, he committed more troops to the defence of Norway, tying up in excess of three hundred thousand troops, plus additional Luftwaffe and Naval units, keeping them there for the rest of the war. Who knows what that decision cost the Germans when they began to suffer defeats in other theatres of the war.

Durnford-Slater recalls the Hampden bomber (of 50 Sqn) dropping a smoke bomb on my father's landing craft, which my father wrongly identifies as a Beaufighter. Given the difficulties of identifying aircraft while at the same time as trying to escape from a burning landing craft, I think my father can be forgiven for that mistake.

Once ashore my father seems to have fallen victim to his own modesty once again. At my father's funeral I was approached by one of his former comrades from 3 Commando who gave me a slightly different account of events. I'm afraid I can't remember his name, so I'll call him Alf for the purposes of this story. This is his version of events.

The scene: The two of them, lying with other survivors from the landing craft on the shingle beach, half in and half out of the freezing water of the fjord (it was December, after all) in an attempt to remain protected from German rifle and machine gun fire.

Alf: "'Ere Bob, what's in that haversack you've got wrapped round your chest?"

Bob: "I don't know. The Sergeant gave it to me and told me to give it to him when he asked for it. Why?"

Alf: "Well, you better check, 'cos it's smoking."

Dad checks the contents and finds the haversack to be full of explosives, pulls the haversack from around his neck and throws it as hard as he can out into the fjord.

If that were a scene in a Hollywood movie, the haversack would then explode, sending up a huge plume of water. But it was real life, so the haversack just sank to the bottom of the fjord, where it is probably still lying to this day.

To that small act of observation from Alf, I probably owe my very existence as a person.

I found it interesting that different accounts of the operation can tell slightly different versions of the same events. Durnford-Slater recalls that amongst the prisoners that were taken on Maaloy were two 'Pleasure Girls', Norwegian prostitutes hired to comfort the German soldiers. Once on board the Prince Charles, the two were confined to the ships' medical officer's cabin with two naval ratings stationed outside as guards. Durnford-Slater recalls seeing the two guards attending to their duties with great diligence, despite the obvious temptations within the cabin. He makes special mention of it.

Joseph H Devin, however, cites witnesses that said the two guards disappeared for quite a lengthy period and that there were sounds of energetic activity emanating from within the cabin. Whose version is correct I cannot say with certainty, but with the reputation that the Royal Navy enjoys when it comes to females, I suspect that it is Devin's version.

The exiled King Haakon took a very dim view of Norwegians collaborating with the Germans and the two women were put on trial and given long prison sentences.

As for my father, he was hospitalised in Aberdeen, where he remained until his twenty first birthday in February 1942, before re-joining the commando at Largs. Such a lengthy confinement in hospital for such apparently minor injuries may seem strange today, but at that time anti-biotic medicines were almost unknown. The risk to my father wasn't so much from the wounds he suffered, but from infections that might set in afterwards.

I suspect that the doctors at the hospital knew that if the commandos were discharged too early they would soon be diving around, up their necks in mud once again, so they weren't prepared to risk their health by discharging them until their wounds were fully healed.

It is a credit to those doctors that, as a boy, I was almost unaware that my father had been wounded, because he had almost no visible scarring, which was very unusual for burn victims at that time.

COMMANDOS wounded at Vaagso enjoy the jokes at a concert in a Scottish hospital. ("Evening Express" copyright.)

*Printed in the Daily Record 15<sup>th</sup> January 1942. My father is third from the left, wearing the vertical head bandage.*

*The Vågsøy/Màløy memorial*

There is a very good BBC DVD available called "Great Raids of World War II", which features Operation Archery. It is well worth watching and may be purchased through internet retailers. A rather jingoistic but shorter version can also be seen on YouTube by following this link
**https://www.youtube.com/watch?v=sf9QRpKyUyI**

# 6 – Dieppe

We were still doing assault training. The boats would come along the Clyde, we'd be told to parade on the dock and the assault boats would come along and take us off.

We would go away at for a couple of weeks at a time to Inveraray at that time, our commando would start on its rock climbing courses.

We had a couple of rocks down the road between Largs and Fairlie, which were fairly high up and we would practice on those and it was another addition to our training. And we used to do schemes on the moors at the back of Largs.

They had started up a small mountain climbing section which was based on Glencoe. They came out and instructed a small group of people and senior NCOs at the time and they in turn passed on the instruction to others. Our commando became very adept at it, actually.

All this training was going on between then and our next operation, which was Dieppe. After we stayed there in Largs, it was about June and they moved us down to the south coast, to Seaford and Bishopstone. I actually slept with my kit and stuff on Bishopstone station for about a month. That area was in a restricted area. People couldn't get off trains or anything. People who lived in Seaford and worked up in London went through Bishopstone station but they couldn't get off. So we actually slept on the platform of Bishopstone station.

Fortunately the weather was nice.

We knew something was in the offing, but we didn't know what it was. Of course, we saw the big concentrations of Canadian troops down there.

We were actually briefed in Seaford. It was only time, I think, that I haven't been into a confined area for briefing. We were actually briefed in our little troop headquarters via Troop Commanders. When it (the operation) happened, we went over from Newhaven itself.

Unfortunately, because our commando was good at rock climbing, we drew the left-hand flank of the raid, a battery which was on top of cliffs (at Berneval-le-Grand, known as the Goebbels Battery). They sent our commando across in the actual assault boats, from Newhaven, small boats. No 4 Commando, who went in on the right of the Canadians, went in on the bigger boats then came off with the landing craft.

We were unfortunate enough in that half way across we ran into a convoy of E-Boats (fast patrol boats, known as Schnellboots or S-Boot by the Germans) which wasn't very healthy. Once again, I was fortunate. 4 Troop, which was my troop, were a reserve troop. Once the main assault had gone in, our job was to go in and hold the beach, so that the others could withdraw through us. So they sent us over on what they called a landing craft ack-ack, which had ack-ack (ant-aircraft guns) guns on it, so our troop were all together there. The other troops, however, running into the E-Boat convoy, were scattered all over the place. Finally there was only about a troop and half actually landed, and out of that only about eighteen men managed to get back off the beach and the rest went into the bag (were taken prisoner).

Those boats, that took them in, were supposed to come back for us, so fortunately, once again, my good luck, we didn't see any of the action in the end. We sat on the landing craft ack-ack, once they found out that there was no way in, our commanding officer had his boat shot out from under him, he came on board, and said "We just can't take anyone in. There's no way to get anyone in there now".

He pleaded with the overall commander and said if I do commit these men now, I won't have any remnants of my commando on which to start re-training. So, it was decided and we sat on the landing craft deck all day. We went down to Dieppe then and were used as an anti-aircraft battery. We picked up two of our British pilots who were shot down in the water. Then came back to Newhaven. We arrived in Newhaven about 4 o'clock in the afternoon and were out in the town at 6. It was amazing.

Our ack-ack boats actually sank two of the trawlers that were coming down with the E-Boat convoy. We were actually fired on. This was a bad position to be in. Our instinct was to hit the deck, find a nice position to fire from and to fire back. We could hit the deck alright, but we couldn't fire back. Funnily this leaves you in a void. You don't know what to do. We finally found out we were getting in the way of the people trying to fire the guns, so all we could do was go back down into the hold until it quietened down. We actually had two people on that boat who were killed.

*The return from Dieppe – my father 3rd from left making the rude sign. Also identified: to my father's right are Vince Osborn MM, Vernon Coaker and Fred Walker. The smiles are because they're just happy to still be alive.*

[...] It was one of the easiest things that happened. We just came back, changed out of our kit and most of us went into Brighton for the evening. The only time it's ever happened, when any sort of troops were in action and then back out on the town in the evening.

There were a few days while we waited to see who had come back. People were drifting back for a few days. We had one Sergeant, Sgt (Clive) Collins, all on his own, brought back one of the ILC (infantry landing craft) back, all the way from Berneval. He actually brought it back on his own. He got an MM (Military Medal) for it. *

Then, of course, we had another bout of leave, three or four weeks, then there was a lot of re-organising had to go on, because we had lost an awful lot of men. They moved us from Seaford up to Lewes, Put us into civvy (civilian) billets in Lewes and we started re-grouping.

*3 Commando bathing party in Lewes , Summer 1945 My father is on the left in the unfashionable one-piece suit.*

At that time we took in one of the best intakes from Achnacarry that ever came to the Commando and they were all serving policemen. Up until that time their occupation had been reserved ** and they suddenly said 'now you can volunteer for the forces if you want to.'

A lot of them did this and the Commandos had a body of men used to discipline and big strong lads. In fact when our heavy weapons troop formed after Dieppe they were from these policemen. They were all big fellows who could handle mortars and could throw Vickers machine guns around and things like that. Which at that time

I no longer had any ambition to do. But they were one of the finest intakes that we ever had.

From there we moved down to Weymouth and had a short period there, training. We attacked a couple of airports and dockyards down there (as training exercises) and we helped in the search for a couple of escaped prisoners from Portland prison.

They were thinking that Spain might come into the war and we were posted out to Gibraltar. In case Spain came into the war they already had contingency plans for the Commando that was there to go straight across to capture the gun batteries opposite Gibraltar. […]

* My father's memory is slightly at fault here. Sgt C E A Collins was awarded a Mention in Dispatches not a Military Medal (London Gazette Edition 35729, p4328, dated 2nd October 1942).

** People in some occupations were considered too valuable to the war effort to enlist in, or be conscripted into, the armed forces. These included (amongst several others) coal miners, shipbuilders, agricultural workers, fire fighters and, it seems up until 1942, the police. There were about 5 million men in Britain working in reserved occupations.

# Operation Jubilee

It has been said that the performing of a Grand Opera is a million things not going wrong at the same time. So it is with a military operation. It only needs one small component to go wrong and things can start to unravel quite quickly. Operation Jubilee was a good example of this.

The United States of America had entered the war in December 1941 and they had some different ideas about how the war in Europe should be waged. For a start they advocated an immediate invasion of France. This was something that Britain opposed. The British

High Command understood how difficult an invasion would be and so it proved when, in 1944, it eventually happened. Britain also had other priorities. In 1942 Britain's army in North Africa had its back almost against the Suez Canal, with Rommel's Africa Corps poised to sweep it aside and seize this vital strategic waterway, sealing off one end of the Mediterranean and opening a supply route for Germany to the oil rich Persian Gulf.

America also didn't appreciate the value of the raids being conducted under the auspices of Combined Operations. They were considered pin pricks of little strategic value. Knowing about the extra troops sent to defend Norway after the Vaagso raid, Britain disagreed.

The Canadians, with two full divisions based in England, didn't think that they were involved enough in the war in Europe and were seeking a way to demonstrate their value. A major raid on Europe might offer them that possibility.

The RAF had a heavy influence on the mounting of the Dieppe operation. Their fighters were having to fly deep into France in order to engage the Luftwaffe and were suffering heavy losses because of that. However, a raid on a major port would be assumed by the Germans to be the start of an Allied invasion, which would force the Luftwaffe over the coast to defend the port. They were therefore strong advocates for the raid.

Finally, the Soviet Union was bearing the brunt of the fighting in Europe in 1942 and were agitating for the opening of a second front. As with the RAF's thinking, a raid on a French port would force the Germans to draw troops away from the East to defend against a presumed invasion in the West.

It was against this complicated backdrop that Churchill approved the raid on Dieppe, codenamed Operation Jubilee.

Conceived as a small hit and run raid on a mainland French port (it was originally going to be Le Havre), General Montgomery transformed it into a full-scale frontal assault. The raid had originally been planned for 7th July 1942, but bad weather forced its cancellation. General Montgomery began to have second thoughts about the operation and it might never have taken place, but for his transfer to take command of the 8th Army in Egypt. Instead, the decision to go ahead fell to Commodore Louis Mountbatten, Head of Combined Operations.

The primary aim of the operation was to seize and hold the port to show that it could be done, with the secondary aim of gathering intelligence. The attacking force would then destroy defensive positions and German military assets before withdrawing.

The raid would be mounted using five thousand Canadian troops, one thousand British troops and fifty United States Army Rangers. Of the British troops, the majority would be made up from 3, 4 and 40 commandos, with French elements from 10 (Inter Allied) Commando and 30 Commando, who were an intelligence gathering unit.

In terms of its size, the raid was too big for a hit and run attack and too small for a major assault. The naval support, while generous, didn't contain any capital ships, reducing the effective fire power of the force.

40 Commando were to be part of the main assault on the port, but 3 and 4 commandos had specific roles to play in the raid. There were two major German artillery batteries to the East and West of the town. 4 Commando were assigned the "Hess" batteries at Quiberville and Varengeville on the West side of the town, and their part of the operation was called Operation Cauldron.

3 Commando were assigned to attack the "Goebbels" battery at Berneval Le Grand about eight miles East of the town. It was mounted behind some cliffs and the skill of the commando in rock climbing, referred to in Chapter 4, was a major factor in determining which objective they were assigned. Their part of the operation was codenamed Flodden.

The success of Operation Jubilee was heavily dependent on the success of both commandos in taking their objectives and preventing the batteries from firing on the ships which would be carrying the main assault force and, more importantly, which would be covering the later evacuation.

After Vaagso, Peter Young was given the task of recruiting new volunteers for the commando. By this time the Army had clamped down on this activity, probably in response to COs complaining about losing their best soldiers. Young was restricted to recruiting from the Young Soldiers battalions *, which would dramatically reduce the average age of the commando and reduce the amount of experience that could be brought in. However, Young recalls that the new volunteers performed very well.

Once back with the commando, Young was given the task of training them for the Dieppe raid. By this time only six of the twenty seven officers in the battalion were from those recruited by Durnford-Slater when the commando was founded. Two had been lost at Vaagso, but several had been sent to North Africa with Layforce **.

The raid took place on 19th August 1942, with the troops departing from the South Coast ports on the night of the 18th. On the one hand it was the greatest set back that 3 Commando would suffer throughout the war, while on the other hand it was arguably one of their finest hours.

In the opening paragraph of this section I mentioned small things going wrong leading to bigger things. So it was with 3 Commando. Because of the risk of air attack, the Germans had taken to moving their coastal shipping at night. It was a regular occurrence and something that could have been anticipated by the planners.

On the night of 18th/19th August one such coastal convoy set off from Boulogne escorted, as usual, by E Boats. These were fast patrol boats similar to the British Motor Torpedo Boats. The Germans called them S for Schnellboots.

The departure of the convoy had been spotted by British coastal radar and reported back to the Admiralty. Unfortunately, this information did not reach the Naval forces carrying the commando across the English Channel, so when the paths of the two convoys crossed, the lightly armed landing craft came off worse. This encounter was reported by an escort ship at 03.48 on the morning of

19<sup>th</sup> August but the Navy thought that the attack came from the shore battery and so didn't intervene.

As my father describes, the commando's twenty landing craft were scattered, with some sunk by fire from the E-Boats in well co-ordinated attacks. The steam gunboat carrying Lt Col Durnford-Slater was also one of the victims and he had to transfer his command to the Landing Craft ack-ack on which my father was travelling. It was this craft that was primarily responsible for driving off the E-Boats as the two escorting destroyers, the Slazak (Free Polish) and HMS Brocklesby, had absented themselves on some venture of their own.

What made matters worse was that the landing craft the Commando were using weren't the robust steel structures that had been used before, they were wooden craft called "Eurekas" (Landing Craft Personnel (Large)) which provided far less protection against small arms and machine gun fire.

Dawn was breaking and there seemed to be no remaining hope that the commandos could make a landing and silence the artillery batteries that were their objective.

What success could be claimed for the night came out of the lee-way granted to Commando officers to act on their own initiative. In almost any other type of unit no junior officer would ever have been able to make the decisions that were made without first seeking the approval of their commanding officer. They simply wouldn't have taken the risk. But taking risks was what the commandos were all about.

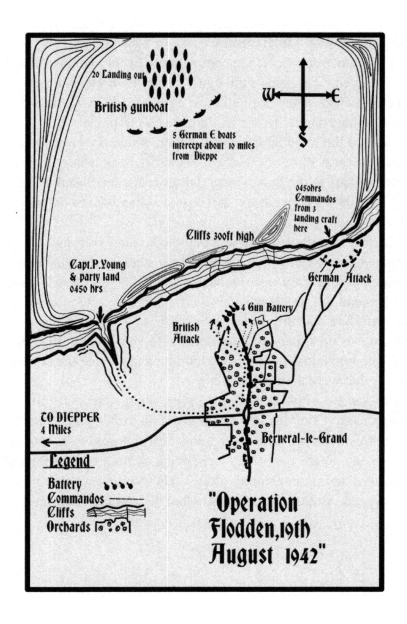

20 Landing out

British gunboat

5 German E boats
intercept about 10 miles
from Dieppe

W ⊕ E
S

0450hrs
Commandos
from 3
landing craft
here

Cliffs 300ft high

German Attack

Capt.P.Young
& party land
0450 hrs

4 Gun Battery

British
Attack

TO DIEPPER
4 Miles
←

Berneral-le-Grand

Legend

Battery ▸▸▸▸
Commandos ─────
Cliffs
Orchards

"Operation
Flodden,19th
August 1942"

Four of the landing craft had escaped the sea battle by
accelerating ahead and closing with the shore. Three of them, under
the command of Captain Richard Willis, the sender of the cheeky
telegram from Lofoten, landed near the eastern gully in the cliffs,

designated Yellow 1 beach, that was to provide one of the approaches to the target. The other, under Capt (later Brigadier) Peter Young, made it to the western gully, designated Yellow 2 beach.

In the assault on the eastern gully, Lieutenant Edward Loustalot of the United States Army Rangers was killed. He was the first American soldier of the war to die on mainland Europe. The Rangers had asked to come along with the commando to gain experience of a real-life seaborne assault.

This eastern force were counter attacked from the artillery battery and came under heavy machine gun and mortar fire before the Luftwaffe began dive bombing them. Only one man, Lance Corporal Sinclair, made it off the beach and back to the landing craft. The remainder, most of them wounded, were taken prisoner.

In the western gully Peter Young and his twenty men fared better. Cutting through the barbed wire that choked the gully, they advanced up it and made their way inland to the village of Berneval Le Grand, before turning back towards the cliffs to attack the battery from the rear. Their advance without being detected was helped by the distraction caused by Captain Willis's party in the eastern gully. During this time the battery opened fire on the main anchorage, but the attentions of the commandos caused their aim to be inaccurate and they didn't cause any damage to shipping.

The commandos managed to creep up to within two hundred yards of the rear of the battery and opened fire. At this time the batteries weren't protected by the concrete bunkers that were in place by D Day. They were made up of earthworks with little protection available between the gun positions and the ammunition storage sites. This was a weakness that Peter Young's men were able to exploit.

The battery commander turned one of his guns on the commandos and started to shell them, but the gun barrel couldn't be depressed far enough and the shells flew harmlessly over the commando's heads. Despite being low on ammunition, each commando soldier carried only one hundred rounds, the commando kept up its harassing fire for three hours, fighting off counter attacks and preventing the battery from firing on the anchorage anymore that day.

*The cliffs at Berneval Le Grand. The route of Peter Young's attack is through the gulley on the right.*

After about three hours the commandos withdrew to the beach to find their landing craft still there, under the command of Lieutenant Buckee of the Royal Navy, who took them off and returned them safely to England. Peter Young and Lt Buckee were awarded DSOs and Lieutenants John Selwyn and Buck Ruxton were awarded MCs.

For a fuller account of Peter Young's involvement in the Dieppe raid, see his book.

A force of less than ninety commandos had taken on a task that had been planned for three hundred attackers. While their attack had failed to destroy the Goebbels battery, it had at least neutralised it for the duration of the operation, saving countless lives. In the raid the commando lost 3 officers and 22 ORs killed. In total 3, 4 and 40 commandos lost two hundred and forty seven men killed or taken prisoner.

In terms of the overall conduct of Operation Jubilee, the encounter with the E-Boats had alerted the shore defences. Although the defenders in Dieppe couldn't know that an assault was planned on the port, they were ready for whatever might be happening out in the Channel. However, the attacks on the two artillery batteries left the Germans in no doubt that a raid was in progress.

The assault on the port of Dieppe came at a high cost to the Canadians in particular. Of the five thousand that went ashore nearly a thousand were killed and nineteen hundred taken prisoner. If nothing else, it proved how difficult an assault on a well defended port was, especially if the enemy were already wide awake. It was a lesson well learnt when it came to planning for D Day.

After the war, archive documents revealed that the job of 30 Commando had been to steal one of the new German "4 Rotor" Enigma encryption sets. Their part in the operation was overseen by a naval officer by the name of Ian Fleming (yes, that Ian Fleming), though it isn't known if he actually took part in the raid. Conspiracy theorists have even suggested that the entire purpose of the raid was the capture of that machine, If it was, it came at a high price.

The photograph earlier in the chapter shows my father and other members of his troop returning to Newhaven after the raid. Their smiling faces aren't an indication of their good humour; they were just glad to be alive. Nor are they making a mistake in their rendition of the V for Victory sign. A war photographer waiting on the quayside had called to them asking them to look happy and show the people of Britain the V sign while he took a photograph. That was their response.

Unsurprisingly, the photograph never made it into the newspapers or official publications.

My father's Army record takes very little account of what happened that night. It reads "Embarked on Commando operation on 18.8.42. Newhaven. Disembarked from operation 19.8.42".

However, it wasn't the most cryptic entry that was ever made in his records.

In terms of what is remembered about the Second World War, Dieppe doesn't feature very highly. In 1993 a Canadian TV film was made about the action, focusing on the part that the Canadian Army played in the raid. However, aside from that, Dieppe is largely unremembered. It is an operation the British wished to forget, possibly because of its association with the King's cousin and uncle of the future Prince of Wales, Commodore (later Earl) Louis Mountbatten. However, that is supposition on my part.

For many years the veterans of 3 Commando returned each year to Dieppe to pay homage to the men lost in that raid, regarding it as more significant to them than D Day. The last visit by a veteran was on 10th March 2016, by former Sergeant John White. He was given a civic welcome.

A small memorial to the memory of those men of 3 Commando that died on 19th August 1942 stands at the top of the gulley above Yellow 2 Beach. A larger memorial in memory of all those who took part in Operation Jubilee is situated on the sea front in Dieppe. In total the commando suffered one hundred and forty casualties that day.


* Young Soldiers battalions were made up of volunteers who were still too young to serve in the regular army. They originated during the First World War when large numbers of underage young men tried to volunteer for Kitchener's new army. They joined at 17 and were given basic military training before being used to guard strategic assets such as airfields, ports and factories. They then transferred to regular army units at the age of 18 for additional military training and full military service. This approach allowed regular soldiers to be released for more valuable service in the field. Stan Scott, whose memories will be recounted later, joined the army at 17 and served in a Young Soldier's battalion. However, Stan also served in a regular infantry unit before volunteering for the commandos.

** Layforce was originally called "Force Z" and was put together with the idea of mounting operations against the Greek island of Rhodes. It consisted of 7, 8 and 11 commandos with a considerable contribution of men transferred from 3 Commando. The formation was put under the command of Brigadier Robert Laycock and renamed Layforce in deference to him. It undertook several operations in the Mediterranean and Middle East. The commando numbers were dropped and they were renamed A, B and C battalions of Layforce. 50 and 52 (Middle East) Commando were later absorbed into Layforce and renamed D Battalion.

*The memorial to 3 Commando at Berneval Le Grand*

# 7 – Gibraltar and North Africa

There was Headquarters and six troops (in a commando). Though Headquarters wasn't a headquarters as you would visualise it. There was very little paperwork done in a Commando. All you had was the Adjutant, the CO, a provo sergeant (Provost Sergeant – analogous to a Special Constable, drawn from the ranks of the unit) and the RSM and a couple of clerks. Those people all became active combatants when you went on a raid. There was very little paperwork done. It was mostly done by word of mouth. People used to pop away and go down to London for briefings and things like that.

But the headquarters wasn't what you would call a normal headquarters. We had a quartermaster, who had two men helping him. The whole commando was probably about five hundred men. Each troop consisted of two sections, which were more or less three quarters platoon size. This was a nice handleable quantity of men (half a section also fitted neatly into a single landing craft, so two landing craft per troop). Each troop had a Captain and two subalterns (Second Lieutenants or Lieutenants). And (the commando had) a Medical Officer of course.

They were meant to be a mobile force, as such we had no transport. Every time we went somewhere the CO had to get onto somebody and say I need to move my men from A to B, can I have some transport and then wait for somebody to provide it. That was OK while we were in England, because he could get us on a train, but as we found out when we got to North Africa he was hitching lifts from all sorts of people.

Most of our time on the Rock (Gibraltar), it was a very nice time. We spent about three months there altogether. The North Africa landings had already gone by then. No 1 and 6 Commando actually went in with the Americans on that. We spent most of our time there actually rock climbing. Marvellous place for rock climbing.

In those days you could get a one day pass (to go) over to Algeciras, in Spain. It was quite a pleasant stay there.

I actually saw Gone With The Wind there, in the Naval Depot.

From there we were sent down to a place just outside Algiers called Fort-de-l'Eau (a seaside area to the West of the city), from which we were then sent to relieve No 1 Commando who had a hectic time in the lines with the Americans and we sat there doing nothing, really, for three to four months. We were doing training, but there was no specific training going on, just rifle ranges, marches and such.

We had very little problem with the heat.

Then they decided that the invasion of Sicily was going to come off and we had one of the funniest journeys that I have ever done. This is where the fact that we had no transport became a bug-bear. The CO was told he had to move his men from there to a place called Attica on the other end of the Med, the other side of Alexandria and Port Said. He had no means to do this. He scrounged transport here and transport there. Some of the stuff we travelled on was nobody's business. And it was all stuff that other units didn't want. They were having so much trouble with it they were happy to get rid.

* We travelled all the way down to Tripoli in this sort of make shift convoy. Then they decided they'd got a couple of trains running and so they decided to put us on a train.

So we spent the next two days going on a train to the other end of the Mediterranean where we went into a very hot place, Attica**. The ground was all boulders, round boulders. This is where they started our training for Sicily.

It was a terrible place to be. In the afternoon huge winds would come up, sand went everywhere. So all our training was done starting about six in the morning. Which was a good thing because of the heat.

We practiced all our Sicily landings down there. The actual areas were marked out on these big cobbles. They built a sort of gun emplacement here and a gun emplacement there, and an artillery battery, which was going to be our target when we landed.

We spent our time there just practicing and practicing and practicing.

* Brigadier Durnford-Slater recalls this journey slightly differently, which is covered in more detail below.

** After considerable poring over maps, and a single reference to Suez by Peter Young (see Bibliography) I established that the correct name for this place is El Ataka, on the Gulf of Suez at the north end of the Red Sea. It has now been absorbed into the environs of the city of Suez.

# A Quieter Time

Whoever holds the Rock of Gibraltar holds the keys to the Mediterranean Sea and Britain had held it since 1704. It was formally ceded to Britain under the Treaty of Utrecht in 1713. With the British also in control of the Suez Canal it meant that Germany had no sea route to the East that didn't involve the lengthy passage around the cape of Good Hope through seas dominated by the Royal Navy.

The British government was worried about two possible scenarios. The first was that Germany might invade Spain, as they had France, and seize Gibraltar. The other was that Spain, under the fascist General Franco, would ally itself with Germany and declare war on Britain and then attempt to seize the Rock. In 1941 there had been a German plan, codenamed Operation Felix, to attack and seize the rock with Spain's connivance, but with a new emphasis on the war against Russia the plan was first postponed and then abandoned.

Despite this, Gibraltar did come under regular air attacks by Italian aircraft and was also the target for Italian frogmen on more than one occasion. In all, these underwater operations sank two tankers and twelve other ships during the period 21st August 1940 to

3rd August 1943. The Italian frogmen were extremely brave and several died carrying out these operations and others like them.

The defence of this spit of land, covering barely six square kilometres, was considered vital by Britain. It was protected by a considerable naval force and fighter planes, along with several thousand troops.

Several commandos had served in Gibraltar and 3 Commando replaced 9 Commando, who moved on to North Africa. The role of the commandos, in the event of an attack by either Spain or Germany, was to attack shore batteries that could be used to fire both on shipping and on the rock itself. The commando spent most of its time practicing for those sorts of assaults and when they weren't doing that they were honing their climbing skills on the sheer sides of the Rock.

According to my father's records, the commando wasn't stationed on the Rock for long, so either his recollection of being there for three months is faulty, or perhaps his records are incorrect. According to my father's records they disembarked on 8th March 1943 and embarked for North Africa again on 10th April 1943, having been relieved by 2 Commando. They disembarked at Algiers on 14th April, which seems like a very long transit time for a relatively short crossing, but it appears that the landing ship Princess Emma took them to Oran, where they transhipped to a large landing craft for the onward journey to Algiers.

Durnford-Slater was not at all impressed with the Army's command structure in Algiers, finding them to be obstructive and slow to act. However, the commando, encamped a few miles to the west of the city at Fort de L'eau, would be largely unaware of the frustrations suffered by their CO. They did, however, find out why they had been sent to Africa: to prepare for the landings in Sicily. Their role would almost certainly be to capture artillery batteries that might threaten the invasion fleet and this enabled them to train for their task.

It was only with some subterfuge that the commando was able to lay their hands on transport. The Second in Command, Major

Charlie Head, convinced a senior staff officer that the commando was earmarked for a top secret mission, known only to General Eisenhauer and the commando's CO. Brand new transport was forthcoming almost at once and in an embarrassingly large quantity.

The provision of transport enabled the commando to train in more remote locations, including the Atlas Mountains.

From Algiers the commando moved by rail to Tebessa in Tunisia. The journey wasn't a comfortable one, with war damaged rolling stock, an unreliable locomotive and an even more unreliable locomotive driver. As can be seen from the photo, some commandos found relief from the heat by travelling on the roof of the train.

*My father isn't in this picture, so I assume he is the one holding the camera.*

From Tebessa the commando moved to Tripoli by road, to take passage in what Durnford-Slater describes as the most rat infested and inefficient ship he had ever known. On its next voyage it was sunk by a German U Boat.

On arrival the commando was told its tasking for the forthcoming operation to invade the South East corner of Sicily, which would be known as Operation Husky. It was to be at a place called Cassabile. The commando spent from early May till the end of June preparing for that operation, as described by my father.

On 30th June 1943 the following cryptic entry was made on my father's Army record. "Embarked unknown destination." The next entry isn't made until 21st July 1943 and the explanation for that follows in the next chapter.

# 8 – Sicily

Then, of course, came the actual invasion of Sicily itself and we found our task went very, very well and what we thought was going to be a hard task was a very easy task.

We had an artillery battery to take out and it was taken within half an hour of landing, with very little resistance. We then were pushed up to help hold the line for a couple of days while the position was consolidated, then walked back to the boats back in Syracuse. We spent a couple of days there.

Then as the small boats came back and went back and the Captain of the landing ship had it dressed over all * and the sailors all round to give us a cheer as we came round. It was one of the most emotional experiences of my life, really, seeing all those sailors. It was a very, very nice gesture.

We had another couple of days there, on board the ship.

The 8<sup>th</sup> Corps (8<sup>th</sup> Army) were moving steadily up the side of Sicily and met some opposition from the Italians and the German army, it was very much a mixed bag there. They pushed us into a place called Agnoni, but we had to move further up to take a bridge at Lentini.

We really ran into trouble on this one.

Before we got off the beach, we were fired at, grenades thrown down, stuff like that. It took us about an hour to regroup once we got ashore, then we made our way (inland) without much problem.

At the same time as this was going on there was a small airborne party **, taking another bridge further on, Primasole Bridge, they were going to drop and take that bridge, which they did quite well.

But we ran into this problem. We were in front of the 8<sup>th</sup> Corps (8th Army), way up in behind German lines, and it was bad up there.

They were supposed to come forward and link up with us. Unfortunately, they were held up more than they thought and, having captured the bridge and stopped it being blown up, the concentration of stuff that was thrown at us, was so much that the CO said right, we're going to have to split up. We split up into groups of three or four and he said to make our own way back to British lines.

He said 'they're in that direction there' and that was all that we could do.

Some of the lads spent about a week swanning around behind German lines, trying to get back. We lost quite a few men there, too.

It was quite an effort. What we didn't know, of course, was that the Herman Goering parachute regiment had dropped during the night, at the same time as we had landed at Agnoni.

They were reinforcing the area as we were moving in. So what should have been a fairly easy job became a very, very hard job indeed.

At one time we had to pack up and leave our wounded in one place with a couple of NCOs and in the hope that the Germans would pick them up. They did actually pick them up and treated them very, very well. Something we were able to reciprocate when we met them again in another little battle (a major understatement, as shall be seen in the next chapter) in Italy. We came up against the same people and managed to reciprocate looking after their wounded, the same way as they treated ours.

I got through myself, OK, though I nearly went into the bag once (made prisoner of war) and was lucky to move out of the way as a German patrol came down the other side of a hedgerow.

There was three of us all together, three of us making our own way back. We always tried not to work on our own, unless we had to. There was three of us working our way back, we were on one side of the hedgerow and a fairly hefty German patrol went down the other side of the hedge and we decided that discretion was the better part of valour and we stayed put until they went past. That was the nearest we got. Other mates of mine were captured for about two days.

In actual fact the German NCO in charge of them let them go (the ones that were captured) in the end because I think he thought with the Army coming up, they were going to have to pull out northwards and he gave them their leave and told them to buzz off. Our lads were capable of making a nuisance of themselves and this is what they probably did and he wanted to get rid of them, I think.

From the bridge it took me two days to get back. We were always wary because we were going back into our own lines but were going in from the wrong side. We bumped into, well, not bumped into, came up on an artillery OP (observation post) and they called up transport and sent us back to their headquarters, where we were given a meal and made very welcome. Of course, we had existed on lemons and things like that for a couple of days, so mouths and what not were quite dry. The nicest cup of tea I ever had was there.

[…] From there we came back and we spent at least three weeks in Syracuse harbour, waiting for people to make their way back. […]

We stayed back in Syracuse for a few weeks. Then they moved us up to a very small village called Stella where we were more or less put in reserve. Once again we were waiting for replacements to come before we could move on.

We had a very pleasant time then, swimming in the Med and what not. There wasn't a lot of training we could do because there was a lot of aircraft activity and the like. So it was more or less a rest camp. Doing a little bit of theory training but not much else. It was a very quiet time.

* 'Dressing over all' is the practice of flying signal flags on a ship from the bow to the masthead, from masthead to masthead and back down to the stern rail. It is a practice reserved only for special occasions or honoured guests.

** Rather more than a small party, as is explained below.

# 3 Commando Bridge

Churchill believed that the key to defeating Germany wasn't an invasion across the English Channel, but through the Mediterranean theatre, describing it as "the soft underbelly of Europe". In that, his opinions had hardly changed since the First World War when he championed the invasion of the Dardanelles as a prelude to invading the Balkans. This time a comparison was made with a crocodile, with the snapping jaws located in France, the vicious whipping tail in Russia and the vulnerable belly to the south. As it turned out, Churchill was wrong and the Italian campaign was extremely hard fought, lasting from July 1943 until the end of the war in Europe in May 1945.

Having defended Egypt against the might of the Africa Korps, eventually defeating them at the Battle of El Alamein in October 1942 and the Operation Torch landings in November, Britain was still worried that the Germans might make another attempt to seize the vital supply route of the Suez Canal. It was the first major land defeat for the German Armed Forces and the Allies expected some sort of retaliation. The only way to prevent an attempt to re-take North Africa was to evict the Germans from the Mediterranean theatre entirely. With Italy allied to Germany, it made sense to eliminate the joint threat offered by both nations by capturing Italy. Any further threat offered by German forces in the Balkans and Greece could be effectively countered from the Italian peninsula.

At the same time, this threat to the southern flank of Europe was expected to pull troops away from both France and Russia, easing the pressure on the Red Army and reducing the number of troops available to defend against the invasion of France, when it came the following year. In the event, Germany withdrew troops from the Balkans, Greece and southern France to use in Italy, rather than taking them from Russia.

This was the thinking behind Operation Husky, the invasion of Sicily, which was essential for the invasion of the Italian mainland.

The American Seventh Army would land on the south east coast of Sicily, centred on the towns of Scicli and Licata. The British 8th Army would land on the eastern corner of the island between its southern most point, Cape Passero and the ancient city of Syracuse. After landing, the two armies would link up before advancing north towards the straights of Messina, the British along the coast and the Americans through the heart of the island.

3 Commando was allocated an objective at the northern end of the landing area, an artillery battery close to the village of Cassibile. They would go ashore ahead of the main invasion to silence the battery and prevent it being used against the invasion fleet.

Durnford-Slater had promised General Dempsey, Montgomery's Chief of Staff, that they would take the battery within ninety minutes of landing. The landings were planned to take place in the early hours of 10th July 1943.

At the end of the training period at El Ataka, the commando moved along the Suez Canal to Port Said, where half of them, under the command of Peter Young, embarked on the troopship Dunera, a modern craft with comfortable accommodation, while the other half boarded the Prince Albert. Liner after liner came up the canal to join the fleet, including a four funnel liner, the Monarch of Bermuda, carrying the 2nd Royal Scots and the 1st Inniskilling Fusiliers.

The fleet set sail on 5th July 1943, under the code name MWF 36 (Moving West, Fast Serial 36).

The journey passed with a mixture of briefings and sunbathing, for there was nothing else to do. Some commandos were concerned about the security of the operation, Churchill having given a speech in which he said that there would be some hard fighting in the Mediterranean before long, more or less signalling that an invasion would soon happen. This breach of security didn't help to calm the nerves of the commandos.

There was almost a repeat of the errors made at Guernsey two years earlier when the sailor in a kayak that had been launched from a submarine to act as a navigation marker, drifted into the wrong position as a result of the local winds and currents, but the error was noticed in time and the relevant course adjustments made to allow the commando to be put ashore in the correct place.

For 3 Commando this was pretty much a bread and butter sort of mission. They landed almost unopposed and rendezvoused about one hundred yards inland from the beach, before setting off across country. This was difficult going, as the local agriculture was based on small fields, each separated from the next by dry stone walls which had to be clambered over. Durnford-Slater became frustrated by the slow pace of the advance and took on the role of scout himself, along with Captain John Pooley.

They arrived in front of the battery and started harassing the defenders with rifle fire, while mortars and Bren guns were positioned to fire into the battery from the flank. The rest of the force circled behind the battery to form up ready for the attack. When everyone was in position, Durnford-Slater's batman, Charlesworth, sounded the 'advance' on a bugle and the attack began. After blowing holes in the defensive barbed wire using Bangalore Torpedoes (long metal tubes filled with explosives) the commando attacked the position and captured it.

Although the whole commando numbered four hundred and thirty men, only two hundred and seventy eight were used against the battery. The remainder were in a second wave, still at sea and almost getting lost. The force under the command of Durnford-Slater overcame an Italian force of four hundred men defending a battery of eight guns. The whole operation was completed in eighty-five minutes, keeping Durnford-Slater's promise, but much longer than the thirty minutes recalled by my father. It was achieved suffering only three casualties amongst the commandos.

After that the commando moved out to cover the flank of the invasion force, before returning to their landing ship, The Prince Albert, the next day to be greeted by the tribute described by my father.

# Malati

The success of the operation hadn't gone unnoticed by Montgomery and on 12th July Durnford-Slater was given new orders.

There were two bridges on the Allied line of advance that had to be captured intact if the impetus of the advance, along the only road from Syracuse to Catania, wasn't to be slowed. The furthest,

Primasole Bridge, would be assaulted by paratroops of the 1st Parachute Brigade, but the closer bridge, the Punto di Melati across the River Leonardo a few miles north of the small town of Lentini, was the new objective for 3 Commando. The bridge was about ten miles behind the enemy's front line, which meant that 8th Army units would have to advance quite quickly if the commandos were to hold on to the bridge.

The intelligence showed no German troops being in the area of the bridge. The intelligence was wrong. The haste with which the attack was planned may have had something to do with the lack of reliable intelligence.

The Prince Albert set sail just after dusk with the full commando on board. Unknown to the troops, doing their personal preparation below decks, the ship narrowly avoided being torpedoed by an E Boat. The captain, Lieutenant Commander Peate, seeing the missile launched, ordered an increase in speed and it passed harmlessly behind the ship.

With no aerial photographs, no time to build models and only tourist road maps available, the briefings given to the troops were far less comprehensive than the officers would have liked. The only rations that could be provided were chocolate, biscuits and tins of bully beef or sardines. The ship's galley provided each man with a packet of sandwiches.

Because of a shortage of landing craft, the commando would land in two waves. The first and largest wave comprised troops 1 to 4, along with the CO and his small HQ. The landing craft would then return to the Prince Albert for the second wave, under the command of Major John Pooley and was made up of 5 and 6 troops. They would consolidate the beachhead, mop up any further resistance and then follow the rest of the commando to Malati Bridge.

The first landing attracted a good deal of machine gun fire, but the commandos gave as good as they got, returning Bren and Lewis gun fire from their landing craft. This was maintained all the way into the beach. Major Charlie Head, the Second in Command, running ashore found himself looking straight into the barrel of an Italian machine gun. He kicked it over and its crew promptly surrendered, too stunned to realise that the Major had been unable to draw his service revolver and was effectively unarmed.

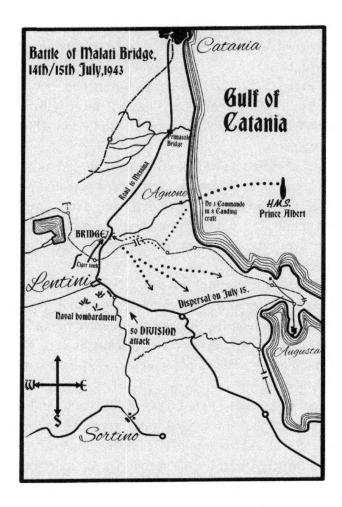

Most of what will now be described comes from the recollections of Lieutenant (later Major) John Erskine, an Australian serving with 3 Commando. He commanded one the two sections of 4 Troop, the troop in which my father was serving at the time.

*Lieutenant John Channon Erskine*

The troop landed with only a small amount of opposition from machine guns mounted in pill boxes. These were soon silenced and Erskine located a gap in the wire next to a pillbox by which the commando could leave the beach, having first eliminated the threat from the pill box itself. The commandos then started a six-mile speed march towards their objective; just the sort of thing they had been trained for at Achnacarry.

They headed inland for about a mile until they encountered the Syracuse to Catania railway line. They had just reached the railway line when the Erskine was surprised to see paratroops dropping from the sky to either side. The ones to the right (the seaward side) turned out be British, dropped in the wrong location for the assault on Primasole Bridge, but on the left they were German, flown in from France to bolster the defences. The crews of the aircraft dropping the two different forces must have been visible to each other. It is possible that the crew of the British plane thought they were in the correct location, fooled by the presence of the German planes, which may be why they dropped the paratroops there.

It was decided that capturing the primary objective, Malati Bridge, made it inadvisable to try to engage the German paratroops, so they were allowed to go on their way unmolested. They may not even have known how close to the commando force they had been. The British paratroops had the embarrassment of having to check their position with Lt Col Durnford-Slater, before heading off towards their objective, fifteen miles away, on foot.

The advance continued along the railway line to Agnoni railway station, which had been captured by 3 Troop, who had taken a different path from the beach. 4 Troop then continued to lead the advance until the railway line passed through a tunnel, which would have been a death trap if the enemy started to fire through it. The commandos opted to take a safer route over the hills to cross the River Leonardo before making their final advance on the northern end of Malati Bridge.

There were only a handful of Italian soldiers to overcome, estimated at platoon strength (about twenty four men) under the command of an officer. This was no opposition for the commando. John Erskine then led a handful of men across the bridge to seize the pill box on the southern side.

3 Troop, when they arrived, were given the task of going under the bridge to remove the explosives that had been placed there to demolish the bridge before it could fall into Allied hands. They later became pinned down there when the Germans started their counter attack.

*Malati Bridge - The pill box seized by Erskine and his men.*

The first German opposition to appear was in the form of an ammunition truck and trailer, heading south towards Lentini. It was hit by a PIAT (Projectile, Infantry, Anti-tank) and started to explode, the detonations going on for several minutes and lighting up the sky like a fireworks display.

It was shortly after this that Erskine and his men first came into contact with the German paratroops, as they spotted about a hundred of them closing on the bridge from the south, no doubt trying to secure the vital supply route to their own front line. Had Erskine decided not to cross the river and had attacked the southern end of the bridge first, the troop would have walked straight into this force.

It was also at this point that the commando found out that there were German tanks in the area. In all, three Tiger tanks were used in the counterattack, however, in the early stages there was only one tank present. The attentions of the tank accounted for many of the casualties suffered by the commando in this operation.

The Tiger was particularly good at destroying pill boxes, which many of the commandos were using as refuges, causing the majority of the casualties that were suffered. For some reason the Tiger didn't destroy the pill box on the bridge which, as the photo demonstrates, remained intact throughout the conflict. The machine gun on the Tiger tank was deadly if it caught the commandos in the open. Erskine had his backpack shredded by machine gun fire, while taking cover, but escaped without injury. His greatest regret during the raid, he says, was the loss of his razor, which was in the pack.

The PIAT weapons that the commandos had were pretty ineffective against the Tiger unless fired from the side and within a ten-yard range. With the majority of the commandos on the north bank of the river and the tank on the south, this optimum firing position couldn't be achieved.

Faced with the strength of enemy that were arrayed against him, Erskine had no alternative but to order his troop to retreat across the river to join the rest of the commando on the north bank.

The whole commando was then forced to retreat as they didn't have the weaponry necessary to take on tanks and there was no way that 50th (Northumberland) Division, the vanguard of 8th Army and still ten miles away on the other side of Lentini, would be able to reach them in time, the deadline for their arrival having already passed without any sign of them.

Durnford-Slater ordered his men to take up defensive positions on the top of a ridge behind the bridge and in an orange grove. The troops withdrew in good order, keeping good spacing between them to avoid being hit by artillery fire or mortars. From there the Commando was still able to keep up harassing fire on traffic using the bridge and several vehicles were hit trying to cross it.

It was from this position, under threat from tanks and paratroops, that Durnford-Slater gave the 'every man for himself' order and the commando split up into small groups to attempt to reach Augusta, a small coastal village on a peninsula, south of the commando's landing beach at Agnone. He could have ordered his commando to surrender, but that wasn't the commando way. While they could still fight, they would.

While Durnford-Slater gave his order for withdrawal in order to save as many of his command as possible, it probably had more beneficial results than he could have expected. Having over two hundred well trained and motivated British soldiers in the rear of their lines probably made the Germans feel very insecure and caused them to commit considerably more resources to hunting for them than they might normally have done. They also served as a distraction from the more serious events that were in progress around the town of Lentini.

As described by my father, the commando spent the next couple of days hiding from the Germans while trying to make their way back to the British front line. Many were captured, but most of them subsequently escaped or were later liberated. Of the nine officers who were taken, only one failed to escape; Lt W F Pienaar, a South African, died of his wounds. As well as Erskine, three other officers escaped while still in Sicily.. Roy Westley, Michael Woyodvodsky and Charles Buswell broke out of a train carrying them through the Brenner Pass (the border crossing between Austria and Italy) and made their way six hundred miles back through German occupied territory to re-join the commando in Italy. Peter Long broke out of his prison camp in the middle of Germany and made his way back to Britain via the Pyrenees and Gibraltar.

Peter Young decided that, as he was behind enemy lines already, he might as well use his position to harass the enemy as they tried to use the bridge to re-supply their front line. Gathering stragglers as he went, he assembled a small force and took it along the valley of the Leonardo towards the bridge. After resting up for a while he found that 50th Division had finally caught up with them. He met up with a party from the Northumberland Hussars, who provided him and his party with some rations before Young and his group moved back to join up with the bulk of the advancing force. Other groups engaged the enemy when they could. Even small groups managed to take

Italian prisoners and destroy weapons and positions that might threaten the advance of 50th Division.

Four commandos came across a much larger number of Italian soldiers cooking their lunch outside a farmhouse. They took them prisoner and stripped them of their weapons, which they threw down a well. But they couldn't guard so many men and sent them on their way, before eating their Italians' food and then moving on before the Italians could return with reinforcements.

Erskine and seven of his remaining men were captured by paratroops and were treated decently enough by the Germans, given the circumstances. When the British 50th Division caught up, Erskine and his men found themselves in the front line, but on the wrong side and had to retreat with the Germans. In accordance with the infamous "Fürher Order" (See Appendix B) with regard to captured commandos, Erskine and his remaining sergeant were actually threatened with death when an SS officer turned up. However, Erskine was able to persuade the CO of the paratroops that this would be a bad idea, given that the Germans were in the process of being surrounded by the British and an execution of that sort would be bound to come to light and the German would be put on trial as a war criminal.

Later that night Erskine and his men managed to evade the SS Officer that was so intent on having them shot, they escaped from the house in which they were being held and found their way to Allied lines. Montgomery asked to meet him and Erskine's main concern at the time was that, having lost his razor, he had to report without having shaved for two days.

It later turned out that in a narrow stretch of land some that separated Malati Bridge from the beaches, the following German troops were operating:

The 1st Parachute Regiment (the ones Erskine had witnessed dropping)
3 Battalions of the Panzer Grenadier Regiment Koerner.
Tanks and self-propelled guns of the Herman Goering Division.

Tanks of the 101st Italian Tank Battalion.
No 904 Fortress Battalion.

A conservative estimate would place that at about three thousand troops. While the presence of the paratroops couldn't be anticipated, the remainder represented a considerable force which Allied intelligence had failed to identify and therefore failed to take account of in their battle plans.

In recognition of the commando's efforts to take the bridge, Montgomery ordered that a stone mason should be engaged to carve into the bridge's stonework the legend "3 Commando Bridge".

*3 Commando commemoration stone, set into the parapet of the bridge.*

The original bridge is still standing, but the main road now by-passes it across a modern bridge.

The commandos were not in the least bit bothered about having been left out on such a limb. Once they had returned to the landing ship after the Cassibile operation they knew that they had no further role to play in Montgomery's battle plan, so while their attack on

Malati Bridge may have been a gamble it was one they were keen to take. Indeed, they would have felt offended if it had been thought that the operation would be too much of a risk for them.

In terms of casualties the commando lost five officers and twenty five ORs killed and four officers and sixty two ORs wounded. Eight officers and fifty one ORs were missing or taken prisoner, many of whom escaped or were liberated later in the Sicily campaign. The ninth officer taken prisoner died of his wounds and so is recorded amongst the deaths.

As Peter Young remarks in his book (see Bibliography), it wasn't a surprise that so many of the commando were taken prisoner, but it was a surprise that so many had escaped or evaded capture. It must have weighed heavily upon the minds of both Young and Durnford-Slater that if the commando had been less successful in evading the enemy, it might have ceased to exist.

Durnford-Slater received a bar to his DSO, Young a bar to his MC, three other officers were awarded MCs and two sergeants and two corporals were awarded Military Medals.

At Primasole Bridge the 1st Parachute Brigade hadn't fared any better. Initially taking the bridge they, too were, pushed off of it by superior German forces. Because they had some light artillery with them they were able to maintain a defensive position until 50th Division arrived and were part of the force that recaptured the bridge to open the road to Catania.

The assaults on both Malati Bridge and Primasole Bridge were carried out at the direction of General Montgomery, commander of the 8th Army. The intelligence provided was that there were no German troops in the area, only poorly trained and equipped Italians.

Montgomery should have learnt from this lesson, but instead he caused a far greater disaster when he lost almost an entire Airborne division while trying to seize the bridge across the River Rhein at Arnhem in October 1944 (Operation Market Garden).

Again, intelligence reports underestimated the strength of the defending forces and the pace of advance of the ground forces wasn't sufficient to reach the bridge in time to prevent its recapture by the Germans. That story is very well told in the book 'A Bridge Too Far' by Cornelius Ryan and the film that was made from it but, I suggest, the lessons that should have been learnt at Malati Bridge weren't learnt and that led directly to the later disaster.

# 9 – Italy

Then they decided they wanted a couple of patrols to go into the actual foot of Italy before the landings. Our commando sent in four patrols. I never went in with them myself. The boats couldn't get back in to take them off, so they were then stranded and they had to stay there for a full week before they were relieved by the troops coming in. According to what they told me they had a high old time.

They met a group of partisans up in the hills and they were coming down onto the roads at night and shooting up convoys, then hiding up in the hills during the days. The Italians looked after them very, very well and hid them and were very co-operative.

After that we were used as commandos were meant to be used, not in the line but doing small raids and holding on till the others came through and then leapfrogging up the coast. At one time we were working with Popski's Private Army. * A great character that man.

He used to work very much individually, on their own. They sort of attached themselves to us for a while.

We did about four of these before we went into a place called Termoli (on the Adriatic coast of Italy, above the 'spur'). It was a great big railway terminus. The idea was to relieve pressure on Rome, because there was a lot of pressure on Rome at the time (I suspect my father meant Naples, as this was nine months before the Anzio landings that were aimed at capturing Rome).

There was us, 40 Commando, 41 Commando. ** We took Termoli very, very easily, but when the counterattack that came in was nobody's business. It was touch and go for about four days as to whether or not we would be pushed out of the town.

Once again, the Army couldn't get up to us, because the rain had swollen the rivers so much that they couldn't get to us. So we were stuck out there like a sore thumb for three or four days. We took a pasting from everything, German aircraft and artillery and what not. At one time, in the woods outside Termoli, you could practically walk over and shake hands with the enemy. They were so close that at night time you could hear them talking.

They decided to withdraw us back into Termoli and that was the first time that they used white tape. Colonel Young, as he was then (later Brigadier), decided he had to get us back out and it was quite dark at night, so what they did was tape the whole route back into Termoli with these big rolls of white tape, so that we could find our way back in. It was very well done.

After that nearly every time we went into an advance position at night time the white tape came out and a route was laid. It was used many, many times after that and it saved a lot of shouting, this was the thing. The advance troop obviously laid them out for the rest to follow.

Peter Young was with us all the way through from Largs. He was the commander of 6 Troop. He actually took eighteen men up the cliffs in Dieppe and stopped the battery we were supposed to capture from firing for, I think it was, three hours. Just sniping the battery.

They actually got so fed up with our people up there that they turned one of the guns around and fired point blank range at them. But they couldn't get the barrel low enough and so they couldn't hit them. Because of those eighteen men the battery never fired a shot during the entire raid.

He (Peter Young) was the 2I/C of our commando and when Col Durnford-Slater went to Brigade he took over the commando. A very great, a well respected man was Peter. Everybody liked him. He was what I called a 'cavalier type man'. He was great man to work with, always gave you praise where it was due. Never asked anything of his men that he couldn't do himself and if you were in bother, he was always up there at the front with you. A fine man.

After Termoli we were pulled out and went back to a place called Molfetta (just north of Bari). Montgomery actually sent us down there and told our CO to let us enjoy ourselves. We went down there for about a month when, at this time of course the Second Front (the invasion of Normandy) was in the offing and our commando and No 4 Commando, being the most experienced of the commandos, were to form the initial landing Brigade for D Day. So we came home to England, had about a month's leave and were taken down to Worthing. That would be Christmas 1943.

We were actually issued with the ribbons for our North Africa Star (a campaign medal) in the sports stadium in Algiers on the way home. We had quite a bit of leave when we came home, about six weeks I think.

There was no sort of strict secrecy, but we were told that there were things we weren't supposed to talk about (while on leave). I don't think I ever spoke to my parents about anything I was doing. They knew I was a commando and they knew it was out of the ordinary, so they never asked about it. It saved a lot of problems that way. You weren't tempted to talk.

We weren't supposed to talk about matters of training, of course, or formations. The actual formation of the commando, the strength and that sort of thing. Normal training you could talk about (presumably normal military training). No laid down secrecy, you were just told there are things that are best kept to yourself and I think it was adhered to quite well.

* Officially designated No 1 Demolition Troop, PPA. Set up in Cairo on 1942 by Major Vladimir Peniakoff MC (nicknamed Popski). They were a small-scale raiding force that operated in the Western Desert and Italy. They hold the dubious honour of being the only people ever to have driven vehicles around St Mark's Square in Venice. They were disbanded in September 1945.

** Commandos numbered in the 40s indicate Royal Marines, who didn't take up the commando role until February 1942. They were somewhat looked down upon in their early days because, other than 40 (RM) Cdo, they weren't made up of volunteers like the Army commandos, they were just RM battalions that were ordered to convert to the commando role. However, they proved themselves in combat and soon became part of the Commando family. Some of their commando numbers live on today with the present-day Royal Marine Commandos.

# Operation Devon

After Malati Bridge, 3 Commando were given a rest at Lo Bello, just north of Syracuse and weren't called on to fight again in Sicily. Having been so badly mauled by the Germans there was a need to re-organise and bed replacements into the commando. 4 Troop in particular had all but disappeared and the commando could only muster three full strength troops out of the six that should make up a full commando.

It was thought that after both Dieppe and Malati Bridge, 3 Commando had been through the wringer, so as part of the re-organisation, the commandos were offered the chance to return to their originating units if they wished. Only three men took up the offer.

While in Egypt my father was show in his records as being on the X(i) list for a period of just over 3 weeks. This is a designation used to show personnel detached to other units, particularly HQ formations and training establishments. I am assuming that it was during that period that he underwent his signals training, which was to dictate where in the commando he served for the remainder of the war. This photograph of HQ Troop was taken about that time and he is in it.

This explains why my father didn't take part in the raids on Italy to which he refers in his narrative. In all only twenty commandos, in five groups, went ashore, so my father wasn't the only one that missed out on this adventure.

*HQ Troop, 3 Commando, 1943*

By all accounts, the commandos that took part in those patrols in Italy felt that they did a valuable job. It hadn't been planned for them to stay ashore, but their landing craft couldn't get back to pick them up, so they were forced to take to the hills. Resting up by day and harassing the enemy by night was what they considered to be 'proper' commando work. They were assisted by partisans and members of the local population so that they could use tracks and hiding places where the enemy was unlikely to find them.

However, in terms of the intelligence the patrols were able to find and send back, which was the real purpose of the mission, they weren't a success.

Five patrols of four commandos each were put ashore at Bova Marina on the southern shore of the toe of Italy. Each patrol also had a Royal Artillery signaller with a type 21 radio, borrowed from 156th Field Regiment, as their own radio sets weren't powerful enough to send back the intelligence information that they gathered.

The following night Peter Young took another patrol back to Bova Marina to recover these five patrols, but the landing craft he was in stuck fast on the beach and all the efforts of its Navy crew couldn't shift it. Peter Young and the Navy personnel had to retreat to the hills, where he gathered as many of the original patrols around him as he could and set about making a nuisance of himself with the Italian forces in the locality. They operated that way for several days, the invasion of Italy across the Straits of Messina taking place in the meantime, until they were eventually rescued by a passing destroyer, HMS Quail.

Not only was the work valuable in terms of disrupting supply lines, it was also very damaging for enemy morale, as they could never know where the commandos would strike next. A fuller account of this operation may be found in Peter Young's book.

Once the invasion of Italy took place the commando was kept busy with raids ahead of the main force. With most of the roads running along the coast, the enemy only had to set up strong points on a road to delay the advance of the whole army. By landing a force behind the strong point it encouraged the enemy to retreat, because they would otherwise be cut off. The landing didn't even have to be a major one.

So it was that the commando advanced along the southern shore of the 'boot' of Italy, around the 'heel' and along the Adriatic coast as far as Bari, about half way between the 'heel' of Italy and the 'spur'.

The next major objective was to be Termoli, a large town to the north of Italy's 'spur', sitting astride the main coastal road. As well as being a deep-water port it was also a major rail terminus, which was important for the German resupply effort. The operation was codenamed Devon.

Strategically the town was important because it was at one end of the German line formed by the River Biferno. The other end of this line was Naples on the west coast. If the Germans failed to hold this line they would be forced to withdraw, possibly as far north as Rome.

The commandos arrived in Bari after four days at sea in landing craft. They were tired and short of fresh water in the late Summer heat and were not ready for the new operation, so Durnford-Slater had to request a twenty four hour delay to the start of Operation Devon. In addition, a certain amount of obstructionism from the Naval authorities (or at least one naval officer) resulted in Durnford-Slater moving the commando further up the coast to the smaller town of Manfredonia, which hadn't been properly cleared of the enemy. It was arranged for a small party from 40 Commando, who were in the same Brigade as 3 Commando, to move ahead by road to clear the town and the harbour. By this time Durnford-Slater was acting Brigade Commander, though he would have preferred to stay with 3 Commando.

According to Trooper Jack Cox, the commando had by now been reduced in strength from four hundred and fifty men to just two hundred. With Durnford-Slater now commanding the brigade and Peter Young in hospital with jaundice (caught while ashore at Bova Marina), leadership of the Commando fell to Captain Arthur Komrower.

Intelligence showed that Termoli was garrisoned by about five hundred troops of the 4th Parachute Brigade of the 1st (Herman Goering) Parachute Division, who had been among the commando's opponents at Malati Bridge.

At 12 noon on 2nd October 1943 the 2nd Special Services Brigade set sail from Manfredonia for the one hundred and twenty mile voyage to Termoli. 3 Commando was to seize the landing beach, about a mile from the town, so that 40 Commando could move through them to capture the town. Taking the beach was considered to be the easier task, as the enemy usually weren't prepared, so it was more suited to troops that were still tired from their recent efforts. At the same time the Special Raiding Squadron *, also part of the Brigade, would move round to capture a key road junction to the south east of the town, where the coast road met with the road from Naples, closer to the German front line and the direction from which enemy reinforcements might be expected to arrive.

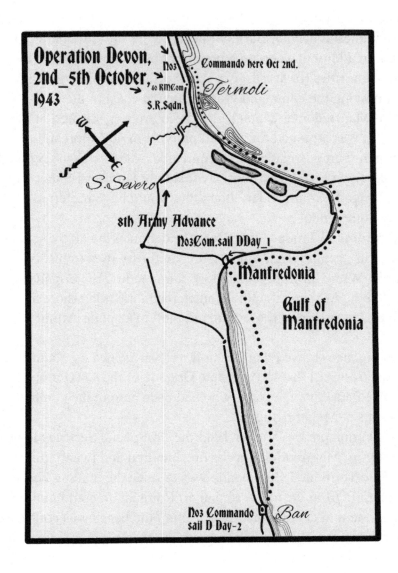

Operation Devon, 2nd_5th October, 1943

No3
40 RMCom
S.R.Sqdn.

Commando here Oct 2nd.

Termoli

S.Severo

8th Army Advance
No3Com.sail DDay_1

Manfredonia

Gulf of Manfredonia

No3 Commando sail D Day-2

Bari

3 Commando made a dry landing without any opposition and quickly established a beachhead about one hundred and fifty yards inland. 40 Commando and the Special Raiding Squadron were then able to land on schedule. By eight a.m. 40 Commando had seized all their objectives, despite fierce fighting around Termoli railway station. Later in the day contact was made with elements of the 78th

Division, who helped to secure the defensive perimeter around the town. However, the town that had been so easily won would prove far more difficult to hold onto in the face of a strong enemy counterattack.

Heavy rain started in the evening, washing away a bridge south of the town that was the only means of road communication with 8th Army. All was quiet for a while until 56th Reconnaissance Battalion presented a prisoner they had taken from 26th Panzer Division. It seemed that the force defending Termoli would soon have tanks to contend with, which again intelligence reports had failed to mention. Unsurprisingly, the Germans weren't going to give up this strategically important town without a struggle. The counterattack started on 4th October with an aerial bombardment by twelve aircraft.

By mid-afternoon the defending force had been splintered by the counterattack with most of the 78th Division troops withdrawing into the town. The perimeter was being defended only by 3 Commando, a troop of the Special Raiding Squadron , a section of the Kensington Regiment manning three Vickers machine guns and one NCO and two privates of the Argyll and Sutherland Highlanders who had refused to withdraw with the rest of their battalion, preferring to stay behind with the commandos to fight the Germans.

Later that night, Durnford-Slater had to admit that 3 Commando's positions was too hazardous to be maintained. In the early hours of 5th October he ordered a withdrawal into the town itself.

For a first-hand account of what then happened at Termoli I am indebted to Trooper Jack Cox of 6 Troop, 3 Commando (and also of the Middlesex Regiment) whose full story can be found on the Commando Veterans Association website.

Jack had been tasked with helping another soldier, Cpl Jack Winser, who had injured his ankle when he slipped down a small cliff shortly after landing. This meant that the two men tended to catch up with their troop after they had been in action.

Following the railway line into Termoli, 6 Troop had discovered a train getting up steam, ready for departure. They boarded the engine and ordered the driver to rake out the coals so it couldn't leave, before discovering eight sleeping Germans on board who were captured without a shot being fired.

There was a fierce fire fight to take the town, but the aggressive tactics of the commandos made sure there would only ever be one outcome. By the time the town was secure the commandos had taken about seventy paratroops prisoner, many of whom were recognised from Sicily. The atmosphere was friendly and there was an exchange of stories as the two sides told of their experiences since they had last encountered each other. Two of the captured paratroopers even volunteered as cooks and produced a passable breakfast.

The German paratroops took great care over burying their dead, according them a solemn farewell. Meanwhile, the commandos were digging holes with a different purpose in mind, the defence of the town. Jack Cox was having trouble digging in the stony soil when a German prisoner walked past, pointed to Jack's half dug slit trench and said, in perfect English, "You would never get away with that in the German Army." Jack Cox doesn't record his reply.

By some freak accident the telephone line to Guglionese, a town further north, was still intact and Durnford-Slater was able to talk to the Mayor through an interpreter. The Mayor reported the presence of hundreds of German tanks in his area, but Durnford-Slater thought the man was imagining things. He was wrong, the tanks were there, belonging to the 16th Panzer Division. Once again the intelligence for the operation had been wrong, as Durnford-Slater would soon find out.

The next night 3 Commando were sent to dig in on a ridge covered by an olive grove, about a mile outside Termoli. This was to be the front line for the defence of the town. Jack recalls the night spent on the ridge as being cold, their light-weight desert clothing offering them little protection against the rain and the October chill.

The withdrawal of the Argyll and Sutherland Highlanders, following an attack by tanks, left the flank of the commando very exposed. 6 Troop then came under heavy shelling, their CO, Captain John Reynolds, being injured by shrapnel but refusing to be evacuated. One of the Vickers machine guns was positioned with 6

Troop and was able to fire at the enemy at long range, keeping them in cover and discouraging a frontal attack. The Germans, however, retaliated with concentrated artillery fire. Fortunately the defenders were well dug in.

When the crew of an anti-tank gun removed its firing block and withdrew from the line the Corporal in charge of the nearest section of 6 Troop showed his contempt for the retreating artillerymen by actually advancing the section twenty yards towards the enemy and digging in again. The artillerymen didn't return, though.

The withdrawal of the nearest troop of the Special Raiding Squadron, who came under intense attack, forced a realignment of 6 Troop's position as they were now the right flank of the commando front line. With the olive trees blocking the ridge there was no attempt by the enemy tanks to climb the ridge as they would become trapped, which was a blessing for 6 Troop. Meanwhile the Vickers machine gun crew kept up a high rate of fire, inflicting heavy casualties on the infantry accompanying the tanks.

3 Commando were now isolated, with no cover on their flanks. Peter Young, who had arrived from hospital and was now acting as Durnford-Slater's Brigade Major, described their position as "playing the part of Daniel in the lion's Den".

However, not even the Vickers could keep the enemy at bay forever and 6 Troop's positions eventually came under direct attack. As the enemy advanced up the slope the acting CO, Lieutenant Anderson (Reynolds had by this time been removed to hospital) gave the order to hold fire. The order to fire was finally given when the enemy were about fifty yards away, each member of the troop having had plenty of time to pick a target. This counter fire sent the Germans, those that hadn't fallen victim to the concentrated fusillade, running for cover and in the failing evening light a series of whistle blasts indicated that the enemy were withdrawing.

More attacks followed, but 6 Troop held its ground and by the time full darkness fell the Germans had ceased their attacks for the night. As with most accounts of that night, Jack Cox recalls the enemy being close enough for their conversations to be overheard.

One German soldier even blundered into a commando listening post while seeking out somewhere to go to the toilet. He was unarmed but holding a wad of toilet paper and was taken prisoner.

Two separate accounts tell of what must have been one of the cheekiest acts of the war. While the commandos showed no lights and lit no fires, some Germans soldiers lit a great bonfire in front of a farmhouse. Troop Sergeant Major King of HQ Troop, a notorious tea lover, sneaked up close on the far side of the fire from the German troops and used it to boil a mess tin full of water for his favourite brew and then withdrew without being seen.

Even though the enemy continued to probe the commando lines throughout the night, the order was given not to fire in order to conserve ammunition. Jack Cox recalls being down to about forty rounds for his rifle, while othesr had even less.

*Trooper Jack Cox, then aged 18*

As dawn approached, Troop Sergeant Major Tony Turner went from trench to trench to tell the troopers to take all their kit and withdraw.

It had become apparent that with the enemy on three sides it was no longer possible for the commando to hold its ground and so they were forced to withdraw into the town. As silently as possible the commando made its way through a gap in the enemy positions, taking their wounded with them on stretchers. As they withdrew, they were passed by fresh soldiers from the 38th Irish Brigade, who had been put ashore during the night from a troop ship. Many comments of "well done commandos" were heard as these new arrivals saw the tired faces of the soldiers they were replacing, marching not in defeat, but fully armed and ready to fight on if needed.

3 Commando went into reserve, based at the railway station. As the Luftwaffe started to bomb the railway station the following morning and enemy tanks appeared, the commandos also saw the arrival of Canadian armoured units approaching from the south. 78th Division had finally arrived in strength; the Royal Engineers having worked through the night to construct a pontoon bridge across the swollen River Biferno. To borrow the words of the Duke of Wellington after the battle of Waterloo, by any objective assessment the defence of Termoli had been a close-run thing.

The cost to the two commandos and the Special Raiding Squadron was three officers and twenty nine ORs killed, seven officers and seventy eight ORs wounded and one officer and twenty two ORs missing.

Jack Cox had lied about his age when he joined the army and was still underage when he volunteered for the commandos. He was only 18 years of age during the Termoli operation and shouldn't even have been serving overseas. He had previously served in 12 Commando and taken part in raids on Norway before being transferred to 3 Commando. He was still attending commando reunions in 2010.

At Monty's insistence, 3 Commando were sent back to Bari and told to make the most of the facilities there, particularly the abundance of pretty girls and alcohol.

That was effectively the end of 3 Commando's involvement in any major operations in Italy. On Christmas Day 1943, the commando embarked for England and the remaining members of 3 Commando disembarked in Liverpool on 4th January 1944. They were granted some well-earned leave before starting their preparations for the biggest sea borne invasion ever attempted, before or since.

* This was 1 Squadron, Special Air Service, established by David Stirling in North Africa. They were renamed to accommodate their new role of seaborne raiders like the commandos.

# 10 – The Eighty Four Days

We had about four weeks disembarkation leave when we arrived home then we all reported back to Worthing. In fact we went on leave straight from the docks at Liverpool and our advance parties went down to Worthing to arrange civilian billets and things like that, for us. So we arrived back in Worthing after our four weeks leave and were given the address of civilian billets to go to and settle ourselves in. That was towards the end of January (1944).

Training stepped up very much so. We were manoeuvring along the coast, opposed landings, we had a lot of exercises with the Canadians who were around that area at the time.

There was a great build up for D Day of course. It was a very, very busy, strenuous time for about five months. Really high-pressure stuff.

We had been told that we were coming home from Italy to prepare for the Second Front, but we didn't actually know where or when it was going to happen. We were gradually getting a better idea from the build-up of troops coming into the area. There were tanks and infantry and transport like the Ducks * and tanks with flails on, which we hadn't seen before and we were very curious as to what they were.

We were used to test troops that were going to have to hold on D Day, so we were used as counter attacking forces. We did an awful lot of amphibious landings along that coast, Littlehampton and places like that. Which proved very helpful later on. We would like to think it also helped the people we were pitched against as well, of course.

We were part of No 1 Commando Brigade (aka 1 Special Service Brigade but Durnford-Smith refused to use the name because of its initials) and we were a strike unit, like we normally were. We thought we would be first in, but it turned out, on D Day itself, we didn't land until H plus one, an hour after the actual landing had taken place.

Our job was to move up to Pegasus Bridge (named in honour of 1st Parachute Brigade, whose emblem is Pegasus, the mythical flying horse) to link up with airborne forces who had dropped during the night. This made a lot of us apprehensive, because of the fact that weren't landing on the first wave, because we were always used to landing on the beach and getting off the beach as soon possible, so that anything that came down, came down on whoever was behind us.

But the roles were reversed on D Day and quite a few of our chaps got quite apprehensive about it.

About a month before D Day we were moved to Southampton - Southampton Common - in the middle of the town, under canvas. They had completely fenced off Southampton Common, with military police, not just our own regimental police, but military police on all the gates and we were confined there for a complete month, going through and being told what was happening. For security reasons we weren't let out.

I was most fortunate because at this time I had transferred from a normal combatant troop to the heavy weapons troop and I was the mortar OP signaller. I was the communications between the actual observation post and the mortars themselves. It meant going forward with either the mortar officer or the mortar sergeant and passing messages back to the mortars themselves so they could carry out their shoots.

Part of the commando training was that you dabbled in a little bit of everything, so they could switch you about whenever they needed to. There was a platoon of mortars in the Heavy Weapons Troop and a platoon of my old friend again, the Vickers machine guns. Two three inch mortars and two machine guns which was quite good support. The infantry brigades only had a company of four as support machine gunners.

During this time they had given us a little bit of transport. Each troop had a jeep for the company commander, a 15 cwt (hundredweight = about ¾ of a tonne) truck for the company HQ to move their stuff around. And a one tonner for moving supplies around or, if we were lucky, moving us around.

As a mortar and heavy weapons troop at Southampton, because we had the collapsible bicycles, which folded in the middle, our troop commander used to get us out on what he called 'bicycle training'. It got us out for about an hour a day, cycling round the town.

*A troop of 3 Commando undertake cycle training.*

As we got closer to D Day everything was closed off, then it was very intensive briefings about what was going to happen. But we never knew where we were going to land. We knew it was in France somewhere and it wasn't until the night before D Day that we found out it was to be Normandy.

Camp life was a bit tedious, but we did have a couple of cinemas, run by the Americans. In fact, going into the cinema one night I heard a Yankee sergeant saying to his mate 'I wouldn't have come over all this way if I'd known I was going to be showing films to a load of Limeys.' **

The camp was actually run by the Americans. All the canvas and stuff like that was supplied by the Americans. The food was English, which I was very glad of because I never really cottoned on to their rations at all. Some things were better than others.

On the eve of D Day we were taken down to the River Hamble in 3 tonners (trucks) and deposited outside the Rising Sun, which is a pub there (it is in the village of Warsash and is still there). It actually has a plaque commemorating the departure of the Commando Brigade. We sat in fields for a couple of hours.

The sight of the Hamble was very, very striking. You could stand at the edge and look down the Hamble river and you could actually walk from one boat to another for about half a mile. It was amazing. All the smaller landing craft for the invasion were mustered there.

Time was dragging on our hands so there was a football match organised between 4 Commando and our commando, then rations came up for us to eat, then they put us on the boats at about six o'clock at night. We must have set sail, probably about seven. As we moved up the Hamble, Lord Lovat (the Brigade Commander) put his piper on the front of his landing craft and got him to play Road To The Isles, or something like that.

As we moved steadily down, huge cheers went up. The people on the banks on either side started cheering. I think it was because, after all that time, something was starting. Not because we were on our way, but because the pressure of at last moving. Being the lighter craft we moved off and formed up outside (in the Solent) because we weren't as fast as the other craft. We had quite a rough crossing, because for about three days before there had been storms. D Day actually had to be postponed because of them. It was still very rough and there were a lot of very seasick soldiers who went ashore on D Day.

*The commandos board their landing craft on the River Hamble*

I was lucky, because being the OP signaller I was up on deck with the mortar officer so I had the advantage of fresh air, whereas the people battened down below didn't. It was quite an experience,

As we came in in the early morning it was quite a sight. As you went in you passed through first the larger vessels of the fleet then the smaller ones. It was like going through different curtains, until you actually came down to the ones that were actually firing. The rocket ships, there was something I hadn't seen before either. They fired salvos of rockets. All the others, the destroyers and such, were firing in support of the troops that had already landed.

From the actual landing on the beach, we should have been able to have gone about half a mile inland before we were on our own, but unfortunately our portion of the beach hadn't been cleared, it was the left (east) end of Sword Beach, right at the complete end of the invasion forces.

We could only get as far as the road, which was about three hundred yards inland, so we formed up there. Lord Lovat moved the brigade through on our own and we more or less had to fight our way up to the Orne bridge where we were supposed to link up with the paratroops.

This was very difficult because all that area had been flooded by the Germans previously and we were about up to our waist in water for about three or four miles inland. We were wading through water with our rucksacks on our back and our rifle. The first things that were disposed of were the folding bicycles because they were absolutely useless to us. They were actually impeding us more than helping us.

The mortars were carried on large frames, called A frames. They were strapped on the back like haversacks. There was a barrel on one, with a couple of packs of rounds, on another would be the base plate, with more rounds. Everybody in the mortar section carried a couple of packs of bombs strapped onto their packs. Even myself, I had my wireless set and two packs of mortar bombs. All the troops that landed had one pack of mortar bombs, which they dumped when they came ashore and they were collected by the beach party who came up afterwards and moved them on.

We came down through Colleville-Montgomery, there was quite a pitched battle there. 4 Commando had swung to the left and with the French troop were attacking Ouistreham. 6 Commando were the advanced commando going ahead with Lord Lovat, the Brigade commander.

We arrived at the Orne and relieved the Paratroopers, who were very pleased to see us, because they had been at it since about two o'clock in the morning. It must have been about half past nine, between nine and ten when we got up there (the commando went ashore at about 7.30 – they had covered approximately 11 km in 2 hours while under fire).

We were held there for a while because the bridge itself (Pegasus Bridge) was under sniper fire and they were very well positioned because they were able to fire straight along the bridge. It took a while to get the commando over because we had to break up into small parties and run across.

We were supposed to have moved to the right, but were moved to the left instead and went towards a place just before Honfleur on the other side of the Orne (this must be a false recollection because Honfleur is about thirty miles from the Orne), but after we got about half a mile we were stopped by the Brigade Commander and we were told that we had to switch and go to Ranville, where the 1st Parachute Battalion were having a tough time and had almost been overrun. So we moved up to Ranville, had a small battle, eased them off and then were pushed onto the high ground to the left and captured a place called Le Plein (near the village of Amfreville) and that was actually where we finished up on D Day, on that line. It was a case of digging in and we then became rabbits for the next eighty four days, living in trenches.

We had a little bit of relief until the following day, when the Germans started counter attacking and it became very hairy after that. They would counter-attack and we would push them back, then they'd come back in again. This kept up for two days, before they left us alone and switched their attention further inland.

The counter attacks consisted of tanks, mortars, self-propelled guns, the works. They were determined to throw us back into the sea if they could. Fortunately, they didn't manage it from our end. In fact they didn't manage it at all, along the whole perimeter.

The following night (I think he means the night of 7th June) there were hundreds and hundreds of planes going over, bringing in the second wave of airborne, I think it was 2nd Airborne Div (Division) coming in to reinforce the line. Of course we were getting pretty tired by that time and we were glad to see them. It was a marvellous sight to see.

I could never do their job though, the parachuting bit. I always felt that you were so vulnerable up there, hanging onto two straps coming down. We could actually see Germans standing up firing at them. They obviously got a lot of support from the ground troops, but they (the Germans) were standing up there firing at them. At least I was on the ground and I could get down and make myself small, but not hanging up there.

Things quietened down then for about two days, then the Germans had obviously built up their forces and started pushing against us again. We had battles on and off again for about another three days. Then they seemed to leave us alone on our front. I think they decided there was no joy in trying to push us out of the way because we weren't going to give. We settled down then to patrolling and harassing them as much as we could. Standing patrols going out at night time, snipers moving out during the day, mortar OPs going out during the day, directing mortar fire onto their positions. It was all active stuff, the idea was to harass them and not letting them settle down.

We were more or less dug in opposite them, occupying the high ground which, of course, was what they were after. He who occupies the high ground wins the battle, as we found out that day.

We actually held the left flank of the invasion force for eighty four days, with the Parachute Regiment, without being relieved out of the line. We were fetched out occasionally. Some of us were sent back a couple of miles down the road so we could have a bit of a rest and recuperation, but we were in the line patrolling for the rest of the time.

There was actually one farm house there, Longmead Farm, where the mortar OP used it during the day and a German standing patrol used it at night. We would go in and we could actually smell the Germans as we went back in.

I don't know what it was, but wherever you went, German soldiers left behind some sort of aroma. Whether it was their food, I don't know, but wherever you went you would always know if a position had been occupied by Germans beforehand. It came in very handy in Sicily and North Africa, because you could tell whether, more or less, if the people out in front of you were Italians or Germans. That was how strong the difference was.

We sustained quite a lot of casualties, No 6 troop were down to about 30 men at one time. They did reinforce us about a month after D Day with people who had been employed on beach parties, loading and unloading, people whose regiments weren't actually over there. They were sent up to reinforce us and sort of help us out.

After about two months we had an intake of actual commandos, who had been trained at the depot. The depot sent us out a reinforcement draft to the brigade and then things settled down and we sat there for eighty four days, taking what Jerry could throw at us and giving him what we could ourselves.

During this time there was a lot of bombing going on at Caen. We used to see the aircraft going over every night. To see so many aircraft in the air, in battle, without any reciprocation from the enemy. There were no German fighters at all, after about three days after D Day we never saw any German aircraft at all.

It was while we are at Le Plein that I saw my first Doodlebug (the nickname given to the German V1 flying bomb). It came over about D plus three. It actually came over the lines as though it was going to England and for some reason, I think it must have been a malfunction, it turned round and went back. Of course, like everyone in England, we couldn't work out what this was. All we could see was this rocket putt-putt-putting away at the back and the sound it was making. But this one never went to England, it turned back and where it landed I don't know (it wasn't designed to land, as such. It would have crashed and probably exploded).

[…] It wasn't our kind of soldiering. We were formed as hit and run troops, being line troops didn't suit us at all. I wouldn't say it didn't suit us, but it was very irksome to us. Our training geared us up to be on the move for the best part of the time. No 1 and No 6 Commando ran into this in North Africa too. They landed with the Americans and they were used in the lines. Which we always felt was a waste of troops who were trained to do something specifically different.

I got the idea that we were only supposed to be in there for about two weeks and would then be pulled back, but they couldn't push out of the bridgehead fast enough so we had to sit in the line. I've understood, from books I've read since, that by holding that end of the line we relieved a lot of pressure off the actual invasion force where it was getting a bit more hairy, up the line. […]

Then the Fallais Gap battle started and as they moved forward and took their little bit of ground, so they moved the left end of the bridgehead forward a few kilometres each day. We used to go and advance behind the German lines at night time then consolidate the ground during the day. Most of it was night work as far as we were concerned. We were infiltrating behind the German lines then holding until the other forces moved through.

As the Fallais people were getting pushed back, so they (the Germans) were withdrawing troops on our front as well. This went on then continuously until Paris fell.

We were put in a little concentration area then and I think about five people from each commando were taken up to Paris to join in the actual victory march through Paris. . […} Unfortunately I wasn't one of the ones who was picked. Something I would have loved to have done, but it was one of those things. […]

After that we were then sent home (7ᵗʰ September 1944).


* DUKWs – an amphibious vehicle. The letters aren't initials, they come from the US military method of categorising their vehicles. Often seen nowadays carrying tourists.


** This story appears in many accounts, so either many commandos heard one American say it, or many Americans said it within earshot of the commandos. Both Stan Scott (see Bibliography) and Peter Young also claim to be the ones to have heard it.

# Operations In Normandy

This book has too narrow a focus to tell the full story of Operation Overlord and its aftermath. One hundred and fifty six thousand Allied troops were landed on the first day, which doesn't include the twenty four thousand paratroops that were landed the night before. Over six thousand naval and merchant vessels took part, of which the vast majority were landing craft. Over fourteen thousand individual aircraft sorties were flown.

To get a better understanding of the breadth and depth of these operations, I would recommend reading *The Longest Day*, by Corneleus Ryan. As well as a wealth of historical detail it also includes interviews with participants and is eminently readable. For those who prefer their wars to be visual, there is also the 1962 film of the book, though there are some scenes which aren't borne out by eyewitnesses (as described later in this chapter).

I chose the title of this chapter because it better reflects 3 Commando's participation in the invasion and the days that followed. It was what happened after D Day that really tested their mettle, rather than D Day itself.

The first wave of the British invasion force were in combat for only a short while before the second wave moved through them to take up the fight. The second wave were then replaced by the third wave until the beachhead was established. After that, however, the units involved rotated on a regular basis. The troops in the front line would be replaced after a few days with fresh troops arriving from England, they would then rest up, often being employed unloading supplies, before returning to the line once again. This established a rotation system that reduced the pressure on the front-line troops, with no unit remaining in the front line for more than about a week at a time.

For the commandos and paratroops on the left (eastern) flank, however, there was no respite. When my father talks of R&R (rest and recreation) he means that some commandos were allowed out of the line for a few hours. Just long enough to get a shower at one of the mobile bath units, a hot meal that didn't come out of a tin (or at least didn't look like it came out of a tin) and, if they were lucky, a film show at a mobile cinema. After that they returned to their unit to allow others to do the same. To be picked for a party going back to Sword Beach to collect supplies was a virtual holiday.

3 Commando were to be part of 1st Special Service Brigade (Durnford-Slater always refers to them as 1st Commando Brigade as he still didn't like the initials), which also included 4 Commando, 6 Commando and 45 (RM) Commando.

The 4th Special Service Brigade landed on Gold beach and linked up with the 1st after D Day, forming part of the defensive perimeter on the left flank of the British 21st Army Group.

Neither 3 nor 4 Commando really liked their objectives for D Day. Both had expected to be used to neutralise an artillery battery or to seize of an important bridge as they had done at Dieppe and in Sicily, neither of which was in the plans.

Durnford-Slater recalls having something of a falling out with Brigadier Simon 'Shimi' Lovat, the Brigade Commander, over this issue. By this time Durnford-Slater was attached to Montgomery's planning staff, with particular responsibility for Commando operations. Lovat wanted to attack a battery some miles to the east of Ouistreham, but Durnford-Slater vetoed the idea because he considered it to be too high risk. If an experienced commando like Durnford-Slater thought that, then it probably was.

Instead, 1st Special Service Brigade would have a mixture of objectives. After landing, 4 Commando would peel left to attack objectives in the town of Ouistreham along with a French Troop from 10 (Inter-Allied) Commando. The other three commandos of the Brigade, 3, 6 and 45 (RM) commandos, would make their way across country to relieve the paratroops at Pegasus Bridge, the vital crossing of the River Orne that the paratroops were required to seize during the night. 6 Commando's task was to open the road to the bridges and keep it open while 3 and 45 (RM) Commando passed through. 4 Commando, having captured its objectives in Ouistreham, would then join up with the rest of the Brigade. After crossing the Canal and the Orne river, 45 (RM) Commando were to move north along the river and capture the small town of Franceville Plage, on the opposite side of the Orne estuary from Ouistreham. I suspect it was Franceville Plage that my father confused with Honfleur, though he would get to that town eventually.

Peter Young, nicknamed *Bungy*, had assumed command of 3 Commando while they were in Italy. The origins of his nickname are obscure. Young himself thinks it started as Bung, to rhyme with Young and was probably first attached to him when he was commanding 6 Troop. The reason why 6 Troop might want to call him Bung is itself lost in the mists of time.

Trooper Stan 'Scotty' Scott joined 3 Commando while they were in training for D Day at Worthing. He was a friend of my father for many years and I met him at my father's funeral. I am indebted to him for his memories of D Day, as recalled in his book (see Bibliography).

Stan Scott was a Londoner from Tottenham and joined the army in 1940 at the age of fifteen, having lied about his age. He wanted to join the Queen's Own Royal West Kents, in which his father had served during World War I. However, he didn't completely fool the recruiters, because he was sent to join the 70th Young Soldiers Battalion, for men too young to join a regular unit. They were detailed for home defence duties only and most of their duties involved guarding key installations, such as airfields, ports and logistics sites.

Scotty did later serve with the West Kents and also with the Suffolk Regiment and the Queen's Royal Regiment. His first stint of overseas duties was to go to Basra in present day Iraq. He returned to England in 1943 but didn't relish a return to the Queens Royal Regiment, who he didn't really rate as soldiers. While in a transit camp in Yorkshire he attended a talk being given by a commando officer, where he heard about the exploits of 3 Commando in Sicily and Italy and decided that was what he wanted to do. In September 1943 he volunteered for commando training.

When Scotty joined 3 Commando he was asked which troop he would like to be in. He had a friend who was parachute trained, so he joined 3 Troop to be with him. 3 Troop was ear marked for parachute training. Although the training started, it wasn't completed due to a lack of aircraft slots. Much to Scotty's dismay, his pal no longer fancied being a paratrooper and had asked to go into 4 Troop. By this time my father was with 2 Troop, which was 'heavy weapons'.

Scotty is particularly valuable in providing more insights into the training that the commando did in preparation for D Day.

*Stan "Scotty" Scott in 1945*

A regular exercise was an assault on Arundel Castle. If landing craft were available they would set out from Portsmouth to land in the Littlehampton area, but if they weren't available the commando would run from Worthing. On the way they would 'capture' the railway bridge and station, then cross the river Arun, which is tidal. It had to be crossed with the tide in, tide out, flooding or ebbing. The perfectly serviceable bridge was never used to cross the river. Sometimes collapsible boats would be used (Goatley boats) and sometimes just a rope which the commandos could hang onto as they waded or swam across. The castle itself was assaulted by climbing over its walls; sometimes a human pyramid was formed and sometimes it was scaled using grappling hooks and ropes.

Transport was always promised for the return to Worthing, but it rarely appeared and if it did it was because there was another exercise due to start. Commandos could never arrange dates with girls because they never knew if they would be able to keep them.

I'm sure the commandos would have preferred the sea landings because the distance from Littlehampton to the castle is only four miles, whereas the run from Worthing was closer to ten.

The commando also travelled to Dorlin on the west coast of Scotland where landing exercises were carried out on the coast of Scotland and the Hebrides using a variety of different landing craft types, with the commandos being based on the Prince Albert, or *Lucky Albert* as she had become known, having survived many bombing attacks in Sicily and Italy.

Then there were the bicycle exercises that my father referred to. Scotty makes them sound far more demanding than my father's narration suggests. For a start the bikes folded in the middle and when opened up were secured by a pair of butterfly nuts. If these weren't tightened correctly, and sometimes even when they were, they came undone, causing the cyclist to crash, often taking the nearest neighbouring cyclists with him. Fortunately, there were no serious injuries. The exercises were also carried out on the South Downs, over steep inclines using bikes that didn't have the benefit of gears, carrying full kit, rifles, ammunition and with mortar bombs hanging from the handle bars.

For several weeks the commandos were taken to Limehouse in East London where the ruined houses and factories, destroyed during the Blitz, provided them with a training ground for urban operations and house clearances. There were several techniques to learn, from 'mouseholing' – tunnelling through walls from one house to the next - as well as blowing walls down and running across roofs to intercept the enemy as he tried to escape.

Commandos from the London area were often allowed home for a few hours leave at the completion of this training, so my father may have welcomed these trips.

It was on one of these exercises that someone had the idea of trying out the 3 inch mortars, which many of the newer commandos had never seen in action. Thinking their range was much shorter than it was, the mortar bomb exploded well outside the training area, placing the nearest civilian population at risk. The commandos never spoke of the incident and it is believed that the authorities credited the explosion to a previously undiscovered unexploded Luftwaffe bomb.

War games were organised on the South Downs, with soldiers from other regiments playing either defenders or attackers, depending on the scenario. If umpiring staff weren't available to adjudicate on an encounter between the opposing sides, such as an ambush, the commandos often decided matters between themselves and their opponents with their fists.

As D Day drew closer, the commando was shown its target for the first time. They studied photos laid out on a map that showed a coastline but which, for security reasons, showed no names of locations. There was a stretch of beach, a town on the eastern side at the mouth of a river and a bridge that they had to reach. The bridge was the primary objective for 6th Airborne Division who would land during the night of 5th/6th June. They would be under heavy pressure from the Germans and it was the commandos' task to relieve that pressure by coming to their aid. The words "You will get to the bridges" became a mantra for the commando.

They were told that the beach they would land on was codenamed Sword and their section of beach was Queen Red. They would not be the first troops to land but would pass through the first assault wave of the 2nd Battalion, East Yorkshire Regiment, which was part of 8th Brigade, 3rd Infantry Division.

The embarkation at Warsash is reported by various sources just as my father described it. The chief enemy at that time was idleness. The commandos were impatient to get going and the hanging around tended to get on their nerves. The disembarkation, however, was another matter.

My father's war record has two short entries for 5th and 6th of June. "Embarked UK". Followed by "Disembarked France". Put that way it sounds more like a trip to Carrefour than the biggest seaborne invasion the world has ever seen.

Anyone who has seen the film "Saving Private Ryan" may think that the Director exercised a little bit of poetic license in the filming of the landing sequences. According to available sources, however, Spielberg may have understated the chaos and confusion of the landings.

Stan Scott recalls the landing craft sailing in line astern across the channel. Going up to stand by the Oerlikon (anti-aircraft) gun he remarks on how quiet it all seemed. Then the landing craft flotilla moved into line abreast for the run in to the shore and everything changed.

All of a sudden the quiet was ripped apart by the sound of artillery shells and machine guns. A Royal Navy destroyer, close by, was split in two and went down. *

The type of landing craft, LCI(S)'s (Landing Craft Infantry Small) that the commando were using didn't have a drop down bulkhead at the front. Instead, the crew extended two long ramps from the deck, lowering them until the bottoms touched the seabed or beach. The commandos then climbed up onto the deck before running down the ramps. Having to climb up and then down left the commandos silhouetted against the sky line, something they had been specifically trained not to allow to happen. As the sailors on the landing craft extended these ramps ready for 3 Troop to leave the craft, one was ripped away by an explosion, leaving just the other for the whole troop to use, making them a more concentrated target.

Next to them, LCI(S) 509, with 6 Troop on board, took a hit from an artillery shell and some of the mortar ammunition being carried by the commandos exploded, but the craft still beached and 6 Troop made it ashore having suffered about twenty percent casualties before even landing.

*D Day – The Commandos go ashore. Note how high they are.*

As the landing craft ground itself against the beach, Scotty's troop picked up their bikes and other accoutrements and prepared to land. Unfortunately some of the landing craft grounded on a 'false' beach, a sand bar some distance from the real beach, and the commandos had to wade ashore through deep water. My father's landing craft was one of those. It was at this point that Durnford-Slater reports that many of the bicycles were lost **.

While the first wave troops from the East Yorkshire Regiment had fought hard, they hadn't made it as far inland as the timetable said they should. There was still a lot of German opposition to be overcome before the beach could be described as secure. However, the commandos were under strict instructions not to stop and fight that battle.

The troop ran down the ramp and hit the beach, only for Scotty to be knocked over by an explosion. Scotty had to be shouted at to get him to his feet as he hadn't been hurt, at the same time as a sailor was fishing another troop member out of the water with a gaff.

Others were being hit by rifle or machine gunfire. There was no one on the beach giving orders or trying to assemble the commandos into their troops, even though Peter Young's description of the beach is of it being organised. However, the commando instinct is to keep going, so Scotty did.

They ran off the beach and across a road into an area that the Germans had flooded. There was no cover, so the commandos just had to take their chances and wade across the flooded ground. Some were only up to their knees in the water, others right up to their chins. Fortunately, the mortar bombs aimed at them just plopped into the water or slapped into mud without exploding. While more men fell victim to machine gun fire, the rest just kept going. Finding themselves on the Colleville-Hermanville road they were at last free of the water and able to unfold their bikes, those that has managed to hang on to them, anyway (as my father said, he had 'lost' his). Scotty and a few others of his troop were amongst those still in possession of their bikes. They climbed on and started pedalling, not stopping for anything, the mantra "Get to the bridges" echoing in their heads.

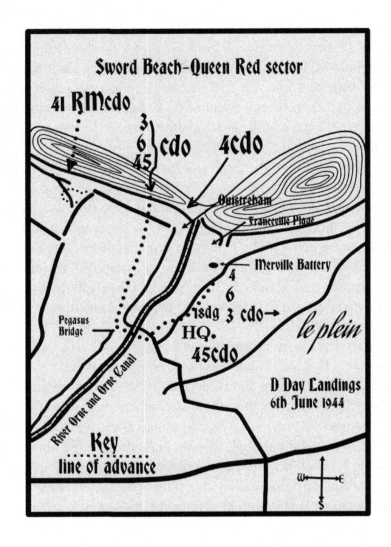

According to the film "The Longest Day", the first commandos to arrive at Pegasus Bridge were Brigadier Lovat and his piper Bill Millin and that Lovat was wearing a white sweater and he was marching at the head of a column of commandos. According to Stan Scott, they weren't even a close second. His account says he was among the first to arrive. This makes sense, as Scotty and his pals were on bikes and Lovat and his Brigade HQ personnel were on foot and would not have been positioned so near the front of the advance. It wouldn't be tactically sound to get the Brigadier killed on the first day of the invasion because he went charging ahead of his command. And Brigadier Lovat was dressed in regulation combat dress. But that's film makers for you, never let the facts get in the way of a good scene.

However, to return to the narrative, Scotty and four other cyclists took cover in a garden about seventy five yards from the bridge, where they came under heavy fire from a building later identified as a maternity home. Two members of the 2nd Battalion, Oxfordshire and Buckinghamshire Light Infantry (the glider borne unit that had captured the bridge), "Bill" Bailey and Wally Parr, were directing Bren gun fire on the building, trying to suppress the enemy's enthusiasm. Stan Scott remarks that he bumped into Bailey again on the exact same spot, but in 1984.

But in 1944, Scotty and his companions lay there wondering how they were going to get across, given that the Germans were firing directly along the bridge.

Someone shouted "You're commandos, get on your bikes and just go for it." (This may have been the CO, Peter Young) They decided that there was only one thing they could do; get back on their bikes and go for it, which they did. Scotty, and troopers Campbell, Synnott, Osbourne and one unnamed, pedalled frantically across the bridge.

Four of the five made it across safely, but Trooper Leslie Campbell (Scots Guards) was shot through the neck and was killed. They crossed the bridge just two and a half minutes behind schedule. Saunders (see Bibliography) records a cycle troop being the first to cross the bridge, lending some support for Scotty's account. Once across the bridge they were able to take cover and fire on any Germans that offered themselves as targets. The rest of the commando arrived during the course of the morning and they had similar experiences of the crossing of the bridge as it remained under fire for most of the time.

Saunders also records Lovat and his piper not crossing Pegasus Bridge until just after 14.00 hours. From there onwards 3 Commando, along with the whole of 6th Airborne Division, became infantry for the next eighty four days.

3 Troop's next objectives were the villages of Amfreville and Ranville, where the airborne troops were having to fend off counter-attacks by the Germans. This area includes the high ground of Le Plein, referred to by father. By the end of the day, out of the seventy five men in 3 Troop that had boarded the landing craft at Warsash, only forty remained. They lost two officers, their Sergeant Major, three sergeants and twenty ORs killed or seriously wounded.

North of 3 Commando, close to Franceville Plage, there was a German artillery battery located at Merville. Despite Allied bombing efforts it was still in action and shelling the landing beaches. The battery had been attacked during the night by the 9th Battalion, the Parachute Regiment, but hadn't been silenced. 4 and 5 Troops were detailed to attack it to try once again to silence it. Hundreds of bomb craters on the approach to the battery provided evidence of the bombing effort. 4 Troop approached from the south and took up a position in a hedgerow to try to provide cover for 5 Troop, who would attack from the east. Little of the battery could be seen, except for four large, grass covered mounds. Although the defenders fought staunchly, taking the fight underground into the tunnels and corridors of the gun emplacements, the battery was eventually subdued and never fired again.

Major John Pooley (Royal Artillery), commanding the two troops of commandos, was killed in the attack and the troops suffered more casualties when the Germans launched a sizeable counterattack in an effort to retake the battery. There is memorial to those who died in the attack at the site of the battery.

The commandos always resented this task. It hadn't been one of their objectives and they considered that the best way of neutralising the battery was to use the big guns of the Royal Navy's capital ships to do the job. However, they did what they had to do, even though it was at a heavy price.

It was 8th June before the Germans mounted a concerted counterattack on the commandos' front line, advancing from their own front line about seven hundred yards distant, pushing through a hedgerow and across a field of cabbages. They were completely in the open and the commandos had no problem dealing with them, once again holding fire until the last possible moment, as they had done at Termoli.

One commando officer considered attack to be the best form of defence. Captain John Alderson took 6 Troop out to locate and engage any Germans in their sector of the line and had considerable success. They accounted for approximately thirty Germans dead, and about the same in both wounded and prisoners taken. Alderson himself was wounded in the knee, but Lieutenant Herbert (Northamptonshire Regiment) was killed almost as soon as he took over command of the troop from Alderson. Herbert was one of several commandos who had been promoted through the ranks to become an officer.

Having been unable to break through 3 Commando's positions, on 9th June the Germans shifted their attentions to other sections of the British line but had no better luck. On 10th June they again attacked the 1st Special Service Brigade sector, launching a three-pronged attack using at least two battalions of infantry, It was the most concerted attack since the commando had taken up its positions, but it was no better rewarded than on their first attempted counterattack. After that the Germans seemed to decide to leave well enough alone and stayed within their lines. What the commandos called the battle for Amfreville was over.

After the counterattacks the commando started aggressive patrolling and that became a major part of their front-line routine. Patrols took place almost every night and a patrol could be anything from a handful of men to a complete troop. First there would be a reconnaissance patrol, looking to see if there was an interesting target that could be attacked. That was usually mounted during daylight hours. The second was a standing patrol, which departed soon after nightfall, getting closer to the intended target and confirming the sighting. Then came a fighting patrol, which would attack the target. Some of the commandos took part in more than one of these patrols each day, using their knowledge of the target gained during earlier patrols. It was June, so the nights were short, but that didn't prevent the commandos from creating havoc in the German lines.

The ideal was to infiltrate behind the enemy lines, so the Germans would be looking the wrong way, then attack them from the rear. There were also liaison patrols, covering any gaps between neighbouring troops or units to prevent any enemy infiltration.

Boldness was a key factor. Once behind the lines the commandos didn't crouch, crawl or sneak about. If they were spotted the Germans would be suspicious of that sort of behaviour. Instead the commandos would stroll about as if they owned the place, hoping that the Germans would be fooled into thinking they were friendly troops.

The snatching of prisoners was always a priority, as they would provide valuable intelligence information, not only about their own positions but also about other troops in the area and even the state of morale. It also spooked the Germans, as they didn't know what had happened to their missing comrades. Had they been taken, or had they deserted? Were they alive or were they dead?

Some commandos would even crawl up to the German positions and try to persuade soldiers to desert, often successfully. Corporal Ernest Lawrence of X Troop, 10 (IA) Cdo, a German by birth whose real name was Ernst Lenel, was particularly successful in this until he was killed during a patrol on 23rd June.

One of the biggest successes was an attack on a German feeding station. Each night a pair of horse drawn wagons would arrive (the commandos nick-named them "goulash cannons"), carrying hot food for the front-line soldiers. With the hungry troops standing around eating or waiting their turn to be served, they made a tempting target. The fighting patrol was led by the CO, Lt Col "Bungy" Young, himself and was a complete success.

On some occasions the greatest danger was from friends and allies. Between the German and British lines stood a farm, Grande Ferme de Buisson, which both sides used as a jumping off point for their patrols. Having narrowly escaped detection by a German patrol, one commando patrol found themselves in the middle of a USAAF *** bombing raid while returning from it and were lucky to escape without casualties.

On another occasion a 3 Commando patrol blundered into an improvised defensive minefield set up by 4 Commando in front of their own positions. Trooper Fred Rabbetts (East Surrey Regiment) was killed in that incident.

The commando positions were subject to regular artillery bombardment, what they called the 'nightly hate'. With so many of the commandos out on patrols they achieved very little, but they were unnerving.

On the plus side 3 Troop discovered the wine cellar of the Chateau d'Amfreville which also housed a large barrel of cider. They drank most of the wine quite quickly, wasting a lot of it as it wasn't to their taste, but the cider lasted them several days as they just took a drink when they were passing.

The accommodation enjoyed by the commandos was primitive, to say the least. It mainly consisted of a slit trench, shared by two men so that one could sleep or eat while the other stood watch. A gas cape (a type of waterproof poncho) might be spread over one half of the trench, anchored by clods of earth, to provide some shelter from the rain. The best constructed shelters might have old wooden boards or doors to act as a roof, which was then camouflaged with heaped up soil. The soldiers heated their own 'compo rations' in their mess tins or, if they were lucky, they were served hot food from a field kitchen.

My father mentions soldiers from the beach parties being used to reinforce the commando and fill some of the gaps in their ranks. However, this wasn't a great success. Most of those soldiers had never seen combat before and hadn't been trained in the tactics used by the commandos. No one held these men at fault for their lack of skills or experience, but they were sometimes seen as more of a liability than an asset.

*Members of 3 Commando relaxing in Normandy*

Scotty's description of his emotions while on a typical patrol describe a cycle. After the initial briefing there was a period of apprehension as the commandos waited to depart, followed by the tension of being alert, ready to spring into action at the first sign of trouble. Scotty describes it as 'expectancy', knowing that trouble was going to happen, but not when or where. Once in action everything happened by reflex: take cover, find out where the enemy was and return fire. There was no time for any emotions at all as they just got in the way. Nowadays we would describe it as an 'adrenalin rush'. After the action was over he felt weary (as the adrenalin wore off), but still had to remain alert as there was no safety until they were back within their own lines again. He rarely mentions fear, but the suggestion is that it was a constant, something to be endured and overcome, but never banished completely.

By way of retaliation the Germans mainly restricted themselves to artillery and mortar fire. When they did counterattack it was in numbers too few to make any impact on the well dug in commandos. The German's main hope was to try to intercept a patrol as it was returning to the front line, but they were rarely successful.

This was the pattern of life for the commandos until 18th August, when they finally advanced as the breakout from the beachhead started (Operation Paddle).

*1944- Normandy - two on the left not known. On the right is Taffy Edwards behind Trooper James.*

As the commandos advanced, they had to be on the lookout for boobytraps. Some of them could be very elaborate. Coming across a German dugout constructed of old doors covered over with soil, Scotty describes the scene within as very inviting. A bed was all made up, even the sheets looked clean. A wonky floorboard concealed a pressure switch and if that didn't work the trap would go off when the blankets on the bed were drawn back. Scotty borrowed several toggle ropes, attached one end to the trap and detonated it from a safe distance.

As with the countryside beyond the landing beaches, a lot of the territory that the commandos had to advance over was flooded, forcing them to remain on the roads, which left them feeling very exposed. One of the weapons used by the Germans was a 'Goliath', a small remote-controlled tank packed with explosives. Fortunately because they, too, were restricted to the roads, they were easy to see coming and therefore could be avoided.

The fighting was a series of spurts between one German defensive position and the next. They tended to use natural barriers, such as rivers and dykes. Each bridge was blown as they retreated, making it harder for the commandos to cross the rivers. Fortunately they weren't wide, but the commandos did a lot of swimming.

The main method of advance was as my father described. There would be a night infiltration through the enemy lines, followed by a clean-up operation as daybreak arrived. They had reached a village called Beuzeville, on the D675 road south of the coastal town of Honfleur, when they were told that the Brigade was being withdrawn from the line.

From Beuzeville they moved northwards to Honfleur. The town, however, hadn't been cleared of Germans. Some soldiers of a Free Polish armoured unit (there were Poles fighting on both sides in Normandy) told the advancing commandos they thought the town was clear, but a commando foot patrol stumbled across a German 88mm artillery gun on the quayside, which fired at them, knocking Scotty unconscious. When he woke up he found himself in a German field hospital back in Beuzeville. Luckily it was now in British hands, though the German medical staff were carrying on with their duties.

My father's service records show that he left France on 7th September 1944, though it would be several weeks before Scotty caught up with him again.

It is difficult to describe my father's personal experiences in Normandy, because he didn't really describe the specific role he held and it isn't described by any of my other Commando sources. However, by piecing together information from a variety of sources,

I am able to give some impression of what my father would have got up to.

The signallers had one of two jobs, which they probably swapped over each day. One of them would be in the mortar position, receiving incoming fire orders to pass on to the mortars' operators. The other would be to accompany the mortar section officer wherever he went, so that the officer had some form of communications with him. This might be a radio set, or it might be a field telephone, the lines to which might be broken at any time and have to be repaired, in the open in broad daylight.

Taking up a position in a forward observation post (OP) they would watch the enemy and the mortar officer would call down strikes on likely targets and report back on the fall of the bombs so that the aim could be corrected. As the name describes, the forward OP would most likely be well in front of the front line, from where the enemy could be observed so that mortar fire could be directed onto them. The OP might be in a hedgerow, a ditch or even in an abandoned building such as the farmhouse mentioned by my father. They would have to take up their positions before dawn, so as to avoid being seen, and would stay there until after sunset before being able to withdraw. D Day was in June, so that meant being out in front of the Commando's positions for over eighteen hours each day.

If the OP was spotted by the Germans, it could expect to receive some special attention in the form of machine gun fire or fire from the enemy's own mortars or even heavier artillery. The attrition rate for forward observers was high. But that didn't exempt Dad from taking part in the nightly patrols. Everyone had to take their turn so as to spread the risk.

One hundred and forty six officers and two thousand two hundred and fifty two ORs had embarked at Warsash on 5th June as part of 1st Special Service Brigade. By the time the brigade embarked for England again at Arromanches (Gold Beach), twenty seven officers and eight hundred and ninety ORs had become casualties. That is a casualty rate of eighteen percent for officers and forty percent for

ORs. Ordinary infantry brigades would have been pulled out of the line well before such significant losses had occurred.

* This was the Free Norwegian Navy ship, HNoMS Svenner, the only ship to be sunk by German naval action on D Day. She was torpedoed by German T Boats operating out of Le Havre. Thirty two Norwegian crew and one Briton were killed and one hundred and eighty five were rescued, fifteen of whom were wounded. The ship's anchor was recovered from the wreck in 2003 and now stands as the "Svenner Memorial" on Sword Beach at Hermanville-Sur-Mer.

** My father's account in his tapes is different from the story he originally told me. In the tapes he says he lost his bike while crossing the flooded ground beyond the landing beaches. He had previously told me he had to let it go when he left his landing craft because he couldn't keep his balance in the deep water while carrying that and the rest of his equipment. Regardless of which version is the truth, he ended up walking to Pegasus Bridge.

*** Peter Young's account identifies the bombers as RAF, but they couldn't have been. The aircraft were Martin B-26 Marauders, which were flown by both the RAF and USAAF, but the RAF only ever used them in the Mediterranean theatre, which is where Peter Young will have seen them on previous occasions.

# 11 – Back To The Front

After the fall of Paris, our brigade was sent home to England, once again to the Worthing/Brighton area and they re-organised us once we got home. Before that we only had three army commandos to a brigade, plus one marine commando.

They decided now that they would change us from special service troops, as we were called then, to a Commando Brigade. They then set us up with two army commandos and two marine commandos. Once we got home, we ended up with 6 Commando, 3 Commando, 40 Commando and 45 Commando, which then formed our brigade and we were stationed along the south coast.

The aim at that time was to train to go out to the Far East, to boost up the commando force that was already out there (3rd Commando Brigade). It was always only a very small force already there.

All the training was based on that, jungle training and such. They used to take us to the thickest woodland they could find. They had to do it that way. There was a lot of simulation. Then there were the speed marches and things like that. They were toughening us up.

We used to play all-in rugby for several hours a day and it was all done on the beach and Worthing beach is all pebbles. It strengthened the legs enormously. It was, once again, a hectic time.

Then, of course the Germans started their Ardennes push (known as the Battle of the Bulge) and the Americans were being pushed back very fast. So they mobilised our brigade and sent us out to Holland and we relieved a brigade of Americans on the Maas itself. During one of the coldest winters of the war, it was a very, very cold time.

Once again it was static warfare as far as we were concerned. Patrolling was very lively. Being winter instead of boating across the Maas (or Meuse in French), in places we were able to walk across and carry on our patrols on the other side. The Germans were on one side of the Maas and we were on the other.

The actual place where we had our first battle before we settled down to sit on the Maas was a place called Linne, which was this side (the southern side). We pushed the Germans out and pushed them back over the Maas.

We found the Dutch people there were very emaciated from lack of food. They had nothing; they were all herded into cellars. I was over there just recently in a place close to Linne where they have a memorial to civilians, a huge memorial and there were nine members of one family who were actually completely obliterated. The youngest one was three and the oldest was eighty three. It was very, emotional thing to see, all these lists of complete families that had been wiped out.

We then stayed on the Maas for about two months, I suppose. We weren't in billets, we were actually in the line; holding the line and patrolling. Which was all you could do because of the weather. We actually went into Linne riding on the back of tanks. It was one of the Irish regiments.

Because it was so difficult trying to dig in, we actually made our gun positions inside derelict houses and things like that, so it wasn't too bad. We always managed to get a good fire going provided it was kept down and things like that.

Then, of course, came the breakout from Holland. We didn't have a lot to do with that. We just held that line until we were relieved by a British infantry division. Once the ground had been taken, we were then moved up to just behind the River Rhein, where we went into position and practiced for the crossing of the Rhein.

We were about two miles back and we worked for six weeks behind a continuous smoke screen between us and the River Rhein itself. The Royal Engineers' job was to keep this going so the Germans couldn't see the build-up of troops behind the river, so the Germans couldn't see what was going on or where it was going to come from.

Once again it was concentrated training. This time we trained in the use of DUKWs, the floating vehicles that could go on the road as well. This was the first time we'd used them and we found them a little bit awkward at first because they were so high off the ground. But once we got down to it, we mastered what was going on.

We were there until the actual crossing of the Rhein. We actually crossed the Rhein at Wesel. The aircraft came across, I suppose, at about twelve o'clock at night (23$^{rd}$ March 1945) and they absolutely plastered Wesel, absolutely plastered it.

We were supposed to go over what was left of the railway bridge but there wasn't enough of it left so we had to do an urgent call for the DUKWs to come up and we were taken across by the service corps (Royal Army Service Corps (RASC) the providers of army transport at that time). Once again a job I wouldn't like to do, ferrying people backwards and forwards under fire all the time.

Being Heavy Weapons Troop we were behind the main assault. 6 Commando actually landed about two miles further down from Wesel and they put out tapes to indicate the route in. The battle for Wesel itself wasn't that great. It wasn't that hard. It had been devastated so much, as I say, there wasn't anything standing on the Rhein side and after a couple of days we went somewhere else.

We captured the equivalent of a Major General there.

We just sat in the ruins of these buildings for about two days while the build-up came in. 6$^{th}$ Airborne came in again, two days after we crossed. They dropped right in front of us and we then became attached to the 6$^{th}$ Airborne Div. We moved out of Wesel with them and we had a two day advance with very little opposition as far as Osnabruck (an advance of about 156 km by road).

We had a little bit of a battle for Osnabruck, it wasn't a lot. Once we got onto German soil they more or less, in most cases, just came out and gave themselves up, except for pockets, like Osnabruck itself where we had a bit of a battle. 3 Commando actually captured the brewery and we were fortunate enough to have with us an officer who had actually managed a brewery in England and after two days he got this brewery going. So we were alright for refreshments, for a while, before we moved on.

Then it was just a case of the British army going forward until they came to a river. We actually did the river crossings for them, held the ground until they came up and came through and this went on right up until the Elbe.

We only had one really bad battle and that was the River Aller. A battalion of the Kriegsmarine (German marines), they were very tough lads. I saw my first bayonet charge of the war there, by No 6 Commando. We couldn't break out of the bridgehead that we had formed. There was woodland the other side and these Kriegsmarine were teeming in this wood and No 6 Commando actually formed up and did a bayonet charge. One of their officers had a hunting horn which he sounded. It was the only bayonet charge I had actually seen throughout the war.

It actually frightened me. News hadn't got back to the mortar platoon that this was going to happen and when this screaming, shouting and hollering started happening, being in a wood we couldn't tell which direction it was coming from. It was very disconcerting.

They cleared the ground and we moved on to the Elbe. Well, before we actually moved on to the Elbe we were in this bridgehead in the Aller and after we'd been there about two days the REs came round with delousing powder and deloused everybody. They'd just opened up the Belsen camp down the road. The news was gradually filtering through to us as to what conditions they'd found in this place.

Everybody was getting very, very angry. We had been treating prisoners as best we could, like we normally did, but I'm afraid that after that the German prisoners got a little bit of a rough handling before they were passed back. Probably not their fault because they hadn't been in charge of the camps, but this was the attitude of the front-line soldiers at the time.

We actually crossed the Elbe into Luneburg and were then pushed up to a concentration camp further up the road. When we arrived it was full of these refugees. Laying out in the bay were two transports that they had brought in to take these away. We suspected that they had partly loaded them before we got there, because for the next three or four days we were dragging bodies out of the actual sea. We suspected they had dumped whoever they had on board before they pushed off.

We were there for about four months, just sitting around doing nothing, except looking after these people in the concentration camp, making sure they were fed and looked after.

# The Beginning Of The End

The term The Battle Of The Bulge was coined by the contemporary press to describe the bulge in the Allied lines along the borders between Germany and Belgium, Luxembourg and northern France. It was the last major German offensive of the war and was aimed at exploiting perceived weaknesses in the Allied military capability at the time.

It was named *Unternehmen Wacht am Rhein* (Operation Watch on The Rhein) by the Germans and the Ardennes Counteroffensive by the Allies.

By December 1944 the Allies had advanced as far as the border of Germany. The northern extremity of the advance was marked by the Scheldt estuary, which lay between Belgium and the Netherlands. Although the capture of the island of Walcheren had opened up the Scheldt estuary, allowing the use of the port of Antwerp, the Allies were still heavily dependent on the four hundred mile long supply route from Cherbourg along roads that bore no similarity to the fast autoroutes of today. The French rail system had been severely degraded in the lead up to D Day, to prevent its use to reinforce the German armies and it was taking time to repair those.

These logistical problems had stalled the Allied advance, preventing it moving into the final phase of the war, the invasion of Germany itself.

It was against this backdrop that Hitler decided to take his last gamble in the west, a surprise attack aimed at splitting the American armies from their British allies and recapturing Antwerp and the Scheldt estuary by the end of the third day, depriving the allies of its facilities and at the same time surrounding the British armies in Belgium. There were two major problems with the plan. The Luftwaffe had effectively ceased to exist in the west, preventing aerial reconnaissance and the bombing of Allied supply lines. The second problem was that the Germans were critically short of fuel for their armour. The film "The Battle Of The Bulge" portrays the German offensive as being primarily for the purpose of seizing Allied fuel stocks, but this isn't the case. Apart from a small number of scenes, this film is not known for its historical accuracy.

However, the Germans had one advantage, granted them by the successes of the Allies. Because of the invasion, the Germans were no longer defending the whole of western Europe and could focus their forces in locations where they would be of most use. This had the effect of shortening the German supply lines. They were also able to use far more telephonic and telegraphic communications and fewer radio messages, which reduced the ability of the Allies to intercept messages that might give warning of the offensive.

The start of the offensive was 16th December 1944 and came as an almost total surprise. Heavy cloud cover kept the Allied air forces grounded and aided the German advance.

One of the hallmarks of this battle was the killing of prisoners, which had been a rarity during the fighting in Europe. The Germans were responsible for at least two massacres, killing approximately ninety prisoners in two atrocities at Malmedy and Wereth, with the blame being laid at the door of SS units. In retaliation it is alleged that there was at least one massacre of German prisoners by an American unit, killing sixty at the village of Chenogne.

For the commandos the consequence of the offensive was that elements of 4th Commando Brigade (it had now been officially renamed from the much disliked Special Service Brigade) were redeployed along the line of the Maas (Meuse) to bolster the northern end of the 'bulge'. That gave the Germans the opportunity in the Netherlands to recapture some of the ground the British had taken. To prevent that, the 4th Commando Brigade elements had to be withdrawn, so 1st Commando Brigade were recalled from

England to plug the gap and defend the line of the Maas in Northern Belgium and Holland.

My father's army records show that he disembarked in Europe once again on 13th January 1945, but this time he was able to keep his feet dry as they landed at the Belgian port of Ostend. Although the German attack had stalled, the battle was still in the balance and wouldn't be declared over officially until 25th January. From that would come Operation Blackcock, aimed at capturing the portion of The Netherlands known as South Limburg, which projects southwards between Belgium and Germany, just north of the Ardennnes.

After being wounded in Normandy, Stan Scott had been kicked out of his field hospital after an altercation with a wounded German and found himself cooling his heels in a transit camp at Arromanches. There he fell in with a with a member of 6 Commando (unnamed). Boredom soon set in and Scotty wanted to get back to England to re-join 3 Commando.

Out for a walk along the beach one day he spotted a troop of SAS getting ready to board an LST (landing ship tank). He and his 6 Commando pal chatted up the SAS troopers and persuaded them to take them back to England with them. On arrival they found they had no money so the SAS troopers held a whip round for them, gathering up a variety of European currencies which were subsequently converted back into pounds sterling. Scotty returned to Worthing via Southampton, breaking many military regulations (going AWOL and stealing a 15 cwt truck among them) along the way without being called to account for any of his actions.

For weeks afterwards Scotty was greeted with the words "I thought you were dead" by all who knew him. Fortunately no telegram had been sent to his mother to tell her about his demise.

Rather than getting involved with the jungle training that the rest of the commando were engaged in, due to a shortage of trained medical personnel Scotty was seconded to the local hospital as a medical orderly, carrying out minor first aid and assisting the hospital staff with routine procedures.

It was while Scotty was working at the hospital that it became apparent that something wasn't going well in the war in Europe, as large numbers of American casualties started to arrive in Worthing for treatment. He was right and his Christmas leave was cancelled as the Commando was put on standby to return to the front line. They crossed the Channel to Ostend on the ferry *The Lady of Mann* before being moved up through the Ardennes to the northern "hump" of the front line.

*Ardennes - my Dad (wearing the beret) and others of 3 Cdo hitching a lift with an Irish armoured regiment.*

When I lived in The Netherlands I remember my father telling me about him being billeted in a convent in the Maasbracht area, not far from where I was living, and how the nuns had been very hospitable and obliging, doing the commandos' laundry and cooking for them.

This story is also told by Scotty, though he does make it sound more as though the commandos played on the hospitality of the nuns somewhat.

There are many stories of the physical and mental fortitude displayed by commandos during World War II, but perhaps the best example is that of a soldier by the name of Walter Selby.

On 2nd February troopers Connolly and Selby had been out in a jeep when they took a wrong turn, ended up in No Man's Land and hit a landmine. The pair split up, considering it to be more likely that one would successfully make it back safely than if they travelled together. Connolly made it back quite quickly, but there was no sign of Selby, who was posted missing, presumed dead.

On 5th February a sniper spotted movement about six hundred yards in front of the Commando lines, a soldier crawling through the deep snow. Thinking it might be a German patrol he took aim, ready to fire. Thanks to the power of the telescopic sight on his rifle, however, the sniper recognised Walter Selby, crawling through the snow. A patrol was sent out to rescue him and he was taken to hospital.

Survival in such harsh conditions was remarkable enough. Selby had survived by eating snow for water, but without warmth or shelter for three freezing nights. But what was more remarkable was that Selby's lower leg had been shattered when the landmine exploded. By all normal standards he should have died, or at least surrendered to the Germans so that he could get medical treatment. Instead he crawled back towards the British lines until he was rescued.

At around this time the 1st Commando Brigade benefited from the attachment of the 1st Mountain Regiment, Royal Artillery, to their ranks. It isn't known if anyone spotted the irony of a mountain regiment being present in one of the flattest countries in Europe, but Brigadier Mills-Roberts (now commanding 1st Commando Brigade) found them at the Hook of Holland, waiting to return to the UK and arranged for the them to be attached to the Brigade. Stan Scott doesn't record what the gunners thought about finding themselves back on the front line rather than on a ferry back to England.

The regiment's 75 mm howitzers * had the advantage of being capable of being broken down into their component parts for transportation across mountainous country. This was tremendously useful for the commandos, who used them creatively to give themselves some artillery support. On one occasion a gun was dismantled, carried up to the roof of a block of flats and reassembled to provide fire support, before being dismantled again and taken back down.

As my father says, that winter was one of the most severe of the war. Stan Scott also describes the commandos settling themselves into the houses along the Maas and keeping themselves warm by lighting large fires – but only in the cellars and lower rooms. The upper rooms were dangerous as they were often the target for German artillery. The soldiers had no winter coats, but they wore leather jerkins under their battledress, which at least kept out the wind.

The hunger amongst the Dutch population was a massive problem, with approximately twenty thousand people dying from starvation. This was felt mainly in the west of the country, when the Germans were encircled, but had affected all the German occupied parts of the country until they were liberated by the Allies, the earliest parts to be liberated being the island of Walcheren and those eastern provinces in the 1st Commando Brigade area. This period of famine was named the *Hongerwinter* (Hunger Winter) by the Dutch.

While 1st Commando Brigade sat on the Maas river, operation Blackcock (14th to 26th January) was clearing the Roermond Triangle ahead of Operation Veritable (8th February – 11th March), which would punch a hole through the Reichswald to the town of Kleve and take the British to the banks of the Rhein. This river was where the Brigade would fight its next major engagement.

The crossing of the Rhein was the biggest operation undertaken by 1st Commando Brigade since the breakout from Normandy. It was a true combined operation, once again, with the commandos crossing the river about twelve hours ahead of parachute drops by the American 17th Airborne and the British 6th Airborne divisions.

While it was supposed to be the first crossing of the Rhein by British troops, the commandos were beaten to the punch by the 51st Highland Division, who crossed downstream at Rees about an hour ahead of 1st Commando Brigade.

However, these crossings didn't diminish the ferocity of the opposition that awaited the commandos.

My father seems to have been somewhat confused by the timelines involved between the arrival of the Commando in Belgium to the crossing of the Rhein. He suggests a period of three to four months passing, when it couldn't have been more than about ten weeks.

Operation Wigeon was launched on 23rd March 1945 and the commando units involved were 3 and 6 commandos and 45 and 46 (RM) commandos. As well as crossing the river, the commando also had to capture the town of Wesel on the northern bank. Some of the commandos would use boats, but the Brigade would also cross in Buffalos, tracked amphibious vehicles capable of carrying eighteen fully equipped troops (not the American DUKWs as suggested by my father, but similar in appearance). Once again the 1st Mountain Regiment were called on to provide artillery support, along with other field artillery units.

To add to the difficulty of the operation, the commandos had to cross while the RAF continued its aerial bombardment, so that they could move into the ruins of the town as soon as the last bomb was dropped. I have to wonder if my father remembered the last occasion when the RAF had been dropping ordnance close to his location, at Vaagso.

The training for the crossing took place at the Dutch town of Venray, where a creek on the River Maas offered a suitable training site. The Commando moved there on 6th March.

When I was stationed in Germany, this small town was only a few miles away on the other side of the Dutch/German border, but my father never mentioned his connection to the area when he visited so he missed the opportunity to return. Similarly, when I had been stationed in Holland, a few years earlier, he had missed the opportunity to visit the Maasbracht/Linne area which was close to where we were living at that time. Had I known about his historical connections to both locations I would have organised trips.

Although some troops had crossed the river during the night of 23rd/24th March, to reconnoitre the landing sites, it wasn't until 21.30 on the night of 24th March that 46 (RM) Commando and the Brigade Tactical HQ crossed, under the cover of the aerial bombardment of seventy seven Lancaster bombers and British artillery. The commandos marked the route with white tape and lights, before sending the transport back across the river to carry the second wave across. It was their job to hold the 'beachhead' while the rest of the commando crossed.

As the vehicles reorganised on the southern bank, 6 Commando crossed the river in the Goatley boats. They were to open the route and guide the Brigade to the edge of Wesel. As 3 Commando and 46 (RM) Commando were loaded into the Buffalos, the RAF carried out its final raid on Wesel. The Army had requested three hundred tons of bombs to be dropped, but the RAF had increased this to one thousand tons. The civilian population of Wesel suffered badly as a result of that decision.

As soon as the last bomb had dropped, 6 Commando advanced, un-reeling white tape for the rest of the Brigade to follow. My father suggests that there wasn't much fighting, but different sources suggest otherwise. They were resisted by staunch defence which included anti-aircraft guns turned into field artillery for the purpose. The commandos then formed a perimeter for the remainder of the Brigade to pass through and into the west of the town.

A lot of the plan depended on the enemy being deceived by the British intentions, so no supply lines were to be set up in the wake of the assault. The troops would have to manage with what they could take with them.

The primary objective for the Brigade was a large factory (used for making wire). Once through 6 Commando's perimeter, 45 (RM) Commando made their way in that direction while 3 Commando spread out on the western side of the town. The factory was to anchor the commandos' defence line around the north and west of the city to prevent it being reinforced from that direction.

At ten o'clock the next morning the airborne assault took place in the face of considerable ground fire from mobile anti-aircraft guns. A daylight drop was very high risk, but to drop at night was even worse, as it risked the paratroops and the commandos firing on each other by mistake.

The commandos were ordered to cease fire during the parachute drop in order to prevent casualties amongst the paratroopers. This was a costly mistake as it allowed the Germans to raise their heads and fire on the troops as they dropped. Many of the plywood gliders used by both the British and the Americans were hit, as were the aircraft carrying the paratroops, but all objectives were seized, at a cost of approximately two thousand six hundred troops killed, wounded or missing out of the seventeen thousand who took part. On the other hand, about four thousand German troops were taken prisoner and many more were killed. It is reported that the suddenness and ferocity of the airborne assault had severely demoralised the Germans.

The air drop had one disadvantage for the 1st Commando Brigade and that was that the artillery bombardment had to be stopped while it was in progress, in case it hit any of the airborne troops. This allowed German troops and self propelled guns to re-enter the city and attack the commando's perimeter. However, this limited counterattack failed to make any progress.

Towards the end of the day the 1st Battalion the Cheshire Regiment crossed the river, opening up much needed supply lines and allowing casualties to be evacuated. Just after dark a Commando patrol made contact with the American 17th Airborne Division, closing the perimeter of the town. Unfortunately, an American officer was killed before the identities of the two parties could be established.

1st Commando Brigade had taken eight hundred and fifty German prisoners with many more Germans killed. The cost to the Brigade had been two officers and nine ORs killed, six officers and sixty two ORs wounded and one officer and sixteen ORs missing.

On 25th March the Brigade moved forward again, maintaining the impetus of the advance through Germany. They would remain the spear head for the advance until the end of the war.

During the assault on Osnabruck the 1st Commando Brigade's Roman Catholic padre found himself going from wounded captive to hero within a few hours. The Reverend Terence Quinlan was returning to the Brigade in a jeep when his driver took a wrong turning, ending up in the German lines to the south of the town. They fell victim to a German ambush.

The padre was wounded in the leg and his driver helped him to a house, where he tried to dress the wound. At which point the fifteen strong German patrol that had ambushed them arrived and took them both prisoner. They were part of a much larger group, about a hundred strong, who were defending the area.

The two prisoners were led through gardens and over railway embankments and as they walked the padre informed the Germans that they were completely surrounded and might as well give themselves up. There were mutterings that suggested the Germans might do that, but two NCOs managed to prevent any attempt at surrender. Seeing that the wounded padre was unable to go any further, the padre and driver were left in the custody of two German soldiers while the remainder of the party moved off into the town. The soldiers led them to a church where their green berets attracted the attention of a crowd of foreign workers. The parish priest arrived and gave the four of them something to eat, informing them as he did so that he could be shot for harbouring the enemy.

After they had eaten, the padre asked his two guards if he was with them, or if they were with him. The two Germans had a chat amongst themselves before laying down their weapons and surrendering themselves to the unarmed padre and his driver, making them the first British troops to take prisoners in the town. They then made their way back through the town until they met up with the advancing commandos. The padre later spotted some of their other captors amongst the German prisoners.

This story of Father Quinlan was reported in the magazine War Illustrated on 25th May 1945.

The Commando did particularly well in Osnabruck. HQ was established in the mansion of a paper mill owner whose housekeeper served up a full English breakfast for the troop. The officer who had been a former brewery manager was Lieutenant Michael Scovell (another commando promoted through the ranks) and he did indeed get the brewery working again. Unfortunately, however, the Commando didn't get much time to enjoy the product before they moved on.

River crossing followed river crossing as the British advanced northwards and one of the most fiercely opposed crossing was that of the River Aller. It was defended mainly by SS troops (there may also have been Kriegsmarine present as well, as my father recalls) and there was a specific reason for this resistance.

Stan Scott records that as the commando approached the river they could smell a really bad smell. It lingered in the air and was somewhat unsettling. When the river was crossed and the commando advanced they found that the smell was coming from the concentration camp of Bergen-Belsen. The SS were defending the river crossing in the hope of preventing the British from discovering the camp while they attempted to destroy it.

The commando wasn't required to liberate the camp, which was still under German guard. With the commando's reputation for ferocity, who know what they might have done to the German guards had they been the ones to liberate the camp.

That unsavoury task was left to the American 63rd Anti-Tank Regiment under the command of Captain Joseph Kramer.

The camp's commander had crossed the Allied lines under a flag of truce to warn of the outbreak of typhus which would threaten both the army and the civilian population if the prisoners were to break out during fighting, so he wanted to ensure a controlled handover from the Germans to the Allies.

Although the commandos didn't enter the camp, the smell told its own story and their closest patrols were able to observe the condition of the prisoners. What they saw would alter the way they treated German soldiers they captured in future engagements.

It was a deliberate policy not to use infantry or tank troops to liberate concentration camps, for fear of how they might treat the guards once they discovered the conditions inside. However, as my father relates, news soon got out and when they were taken prisoner, ordinary German soldiers often paid the price for what had gone on inside the camp.

Scotty confirms the story of the bayonet charge on the German defenders and suggests that it was the last ever bayonet charge made by the British Army that was started with a bugle call.

Following the crossing of the Aller and Elbe rivers, the commandos continued their advance until they eventually reached the Baltic Sea at Lübeck.

The concentration camp that my father refers to was at Neustadt, north of the town of Lübeck and was a temporary one housed in a former marines barracks. The majority of the prisoners were Russians and Poles, with some Jews, who had been brought there from the Neuengamme camp in Hamburg. They were due to be transported (it isn't known where) in the former cruise liner the Cap Arcona and two other ships, the Thielbek and the Deutschland.

The three ships were bombed by Hawker Typhoons from 83 Group, Second Allied Tactical Air Force. The Red Cross had notified the British of the presence of the prison ships in Lübeck Bay, but the message failed to reach the RAF, at least not in time to prevent the bombing attack.

Other than the Deutschland, which had a red cross marked on its funnel, the three ships weren't carrying any markings that would provide protections under the Geneva Convention and so were considered to be legitimate targets. In addition, Allied Intelligence had received information that senior SS officers and Nazi party officials were trying to escape by sea and they thought that these ships were being used for this purpose. The concentration camp prisoners were all confined below decks so none of the RAF pilots was aware that they were on board.

Only three hundred and fifty out of the three thousand concentration camp inmates on board the Cap Arcona survived and fifty out of two thousand eight hundred on board the Thielbek. By contrast all two thousand concentration camp prisoners on board the Deutschland were saved, because the trawler Athen went to its assistance. Other trawlers that went to help the Cap Arcona and the Thielbek only rescued the German crew members. The true story of the three ships only emerged after the war and wasn't widely publicised, so my father may be forgiven for not knowing how the victims he was recovering had died.

The ships had been bombed on 3rd May 1945 and the war in Europe ended on 8th May.

A couple of weeks after the war ended the commando was ordered to Bremerhaven, where they set sail for Tilbury on 9th June 1945 with the intention that they re-start their training to before departing for Burma..

Although 3 Commando were once again billeted in Worthing, some of their training took place in Lewes. It was here that news came through that the Americans had dropped the atomic bomb on Japan and, following the dropping of a second bomb a few days later, the war finally came to an end on 15th August 1945.

Unsure of their future, the commandos continued with their training, but news soon filtered through that commandos were no longer required and would be disbanded. My father's army record shows that he was officially post to the Machine Gun Training Centre, Chester, on 19th November 1945.


* A howitzer is a type of gun which fires a shell in a very high arc to land behind obstacles e.g. hills, buildings, woodland etc, or to explode shells above the enemy's heads

.

# 12 – The End

We were relieved and came home again to England. That was about a month before the armistice was signed. We went back to Worthing again, where everyone was pleased to see us, those that remembered us.

Things were then non-committal. Nobody knew what was going to happen. We started our Far East training again. Then after the victory parades and what not the commando settled down in preparation for travelling to the Far East.

Then they dropped the atom bomb and told us 'you won't be going now'. There was a lot of talk about what was going to happen to us and, finally, we were told that the commandos were going to be disbanded, which was a great blow to us all, because we were very proud of our unit.

It was a bit of a surprise because we thought they would continue with this force and make us an elite force for the British Army after the war. It didn't happen. They decided, Lord Louis Mountbatten had a lot of influence here, that the Marine Commandos would continue in the job. The argument was that the army had taken over the Royal Marines function in the first place. This was what the old type marines had to do. So tradition bore out and the marines took over.

We travelled all the way up by special train from Worthing and were actually disbanded on Victoria station.

There was no parade, we'd had a large parade down in Worthing, Brigadier Laycock (he was actually a Major General by then) came down and thanked us for our contribution. He was very, very upset but politics being what it was at the time, unfortunately that was what they decided.

# Not With A Bang, But With A Whimper

I have chosen to bring this book to a close at this point not because it is the end of my father's story, far from it, but because it is an ending.

In June 1940, Churchill had called on the Army to provide raiding troops partly because he was a former soldier and partly because his good friend, General Ismay, was his chief military staff officer, serving on the Chiefs of Staff Committee. He was a natural choice to get things done quickly.

However, Combined Operations, set up in July 1940, was headed up by naval officers, firstly Admiral of the Fleet Roger Keyes and then by Commodore Louis Mountbatten. Unsurprisingly they saw the responsibility for mounting raids from the sea as being a job for the Royal Navy, in the form of the Royal Marines. Even the replacement of Mountbatten by Major General Robert Laycock (of Layforce fame), in 1943, didn't shift this balance of opinion. The first Royal Marine Commando, No 40, was established on 14th February 1942, followed by 41 Commando later that year and then several more in August 1943, in preparation for D Day.

So, when the war came to an end, the Army commandos were disbanded. There was no parade in their honour along Whitehall and no 'laying up of the colours' ceremony *. So it was on 19th November 1945 No 3 Commando just formed ranks on the platform of Victoria station, were called to attention and dismissed, to return to the units from which they had originally volunteered. A reporter from the Daily Mirror was present to witness the event and to take a photograph.

THE DAILY MIRROR, NOVEMBER 20, 1945

# 300 MEN FROM ENDS OF THE EARTH PART ON PLATFORM 15

"Daily Mirror" Reporter

UNNOTICED among the hustling business crowds, the No. 3 Commando stepped from the Worthing train on to Platform 15 at Victoria Station, London, yesterday and dispersed for ever.

## TWICE DIVORCED, HE STOLE HER CAR WHEN HE LEFT THIRD WIFE

## He broke gaol to see family

*Daily Mirror, 20th November 1945*

The text of the article reproduced above reads as follows:

"Unnoticed amongst hustling business crowds, the No 3 Commando stepped from the Worthing train onto Platform 15 at Victoria Station, London, yesterday and dispersed forever.

Three hundred green berets, representing all that was left of a famous name that exchanged blood for glory in every theatre of war except the Far East: 300 green berets being worn for the last time – their owners returning to the regiments from which they came four years ago.

Nobody recognised them, just another bunch of soldiers.

Victoria Station via Vaagso, Lofoten, Dieppe, St Nazaire, Africa, Italy, Sicily, France, Belgium, Holland, Germany – then the final break up from Platform 15. Their ribbons told of their journeys as eloquently as coloured labels on a traveller's cabin-trunk.

'Cheesed off at breaking up the old unit like this' they all said. 'Busting up the best regiment in the British Army. Never saw such esprit de-corps before. Been everywhere together. Seems funny leaving your friends.'

Londoners, Welshmen, Jocks, Yorkshire tykes, Geordies – all going back to the Borders – the Inniskillings, the Royal Fusiliers, the Gunners, the Guards, the KRRS – the pick of the volunteers going back.

There was one enormous fellow, looking like a six foot hank of battle bitten leather with medal ribbons on it.

'You've been all over the place with the third?" I asked. 'All over the bloody place, chum.' He said seriously, in a cockney accent. 'Worthing, Brighton, Wrexham, all over the place.'

Captain Pond grinned and waved, then they stood alone on the platform. 'Sorry to see them go, 'he said quietly. 'Best bunch of boys there ever was."

Just for a change my father didn't manage to get himself into the photograph, as far as I can identify. I doubt that many of these soldiers would have said 'cheesed off', but it is a family newspaper. I can find no trace of the Captain Pond quoted in the article. His name doesn't appear on the 3 Commando nominal roll, so it's quite possible that the reporter invented the name. Also, no member of the commando would have referred to his unit as "the third". They were 3 Commando – always.

I think my father was personally quite bitter about the way the commandos were disbanded. Having served for so long in such a distinguished unit he felt that more consideration should have been shown for the Army commandos and their achievements. The option to absorb the Army Commandos into the Royal Marines wasn't even considered. As Stan Scott points out, all of the of the special forces, except for the Long Range Desert Group, had emerged from the commandos. The Parachute Regiment had been founded as 2 Commando and even the Special Air Service had been founded by an officer of 8 Commando, Major David Sterling.

By that time Churchill, the inspiration behind the commandos, had lost the July 1945 general election and was no longer in a position to champion the commandos' cause. The new government was focused on rebuilding the country after six years of war and the fate of the commandos wasn't a priority for them. So it wasn't with a bang, but with a whimper, that the Army Commandos marched off into history.

This was rather unfortunate in many ways. Without the shared experience of warfare the returning commandos were often viewed as outsiders in their old units. Stan Scott recalls that he was virtually ignored by his former comrades because he had 'deserted' the regiment to join the commandos. It was only the arrival of some other former commandos that made him feel at home once again.

Many of the commando's contemporaries in the units in which they were serving before they volunteered, had been promoted while they were away and looked on these elite soldiers with some suspicion, especially by those who had enjoyed a quiet war. Some soldiers who had been promoted ** while in the Commandos had their promotions revoked on their return to their units because there were no vacancies available at their rank.

The skills the commandos had developed were largely ignored by both the officers and the NCOs of their units. For many of the commandos it was similar to their arrival from the recruit training depot after they had first enlisted; they had to work their way back into the battalion. The lucky ones were probably those who had been conscripted or enlisted on 'hostilities only' terms as they would soon be demobbed now that the war was over. 'Regulars' like my father had no choice but to take what they were given. Stan Scott found himself, against his will, sent to join the Military Police because of his war record.

My father wasn't even posted back to his regiment, he was posted to the Machinegun Training Centre in Chester. His recollections were of early morning parades and then being detailed off for fatigue parties or sentry detail, as no one knew what to do with him. This was not what a soldier with eight years of service behind him, four of those in combat, should have expected. It wasn't until 23rd July

1946 that he finally returned to the Middlesex Regiment, once more back in Germany.

My father's story went on. He remained in the Army until 10th February 1961. He continued to serve in the Middlesex Regiment but didn't see any further active service. When his battalion went from Hong Kong to Korea in 1951, he was back in Britain deciding whether or not to continue his army service. My imminent arrival prompted his decision to remain a soldier, but it also meant that he wasn't posted back to the battalion until after they returned to the UK.

Later Dad served a three year secondment with the Foreign and Commonwealth Office, in Malaya training candidate officers of the Malay Regiment in advance of their training at Sandhurst Military Academy. Both of my younger sisters were born during that tour.

Posted back from Malaya in 1960, his regiment didn't have a vacancy for a Company Sergeant Major, which Dad was by then, so he was posted to the regiment's Territorial Army (TA) battalion as their administrator. He spent most of his working weeks in the solitude of Enfield Drill Hall, doing the unit's paperwork and organising their weekend and annual camps.

Like the commandos, my father's own service also ended with a whimper, rather than a bang. It is normal for a long serving soldier to retire from his battalion with something of a fanfare. As a Senior Non-commissioned Officer he could have expected a farewell dinner in his honour in the Sergeants Mess and a personal farewell from the CO. But TA battalions don't have a Sergeants Mess as their members are only part time soldiers. Instead, when his discharge was due, he was sent to the regiment's training depot, by then at Canterbury, to wait out his final month while his discharge paperwork was completed. My father doesn't recount what happened on his final day of service, but it is likely that he drove out of the depot gates with no one but the sentry on duty to witness the end of his service.

As the saying has it "Old soldier never die, they simply fade away."

# Sic Transit Gloria Mundi

*Malaya 1954 – Dad is front row, 3rd from the left.*

\* An infantry battalion normally has two 'Colours', flags that once served as the rallying point for troops in battle. The first is the Regimental Colour. As its name suggests, this is a flag comprising the colour combinations used by the regiment (yellow and maroon for the Middlesex Regiment) and on which is displayed the Regimental badge and their battle honours. The second colour is the King's or Queen's Colour awarded by the monarch personally. This is a Union Flag, usually fringed in gold, emblazoned with the Regiment's name and, again, its battle honours. The Colours are treated with the greatest reverence, especially the King's or Queens' Colour. It was a major disgrace for the colours to be captured by the enemy and could even result in regiments losing Royal patronage. When the Colours become old, damaged or faded, when a King's or Queen's Colour is replaced by that of a new monarch, or when the

Regiment disbands, the colours are 'laid up'. This is essentially a funeral service for them. The Army Commandos were never awarded a Colour, so there could be no laying up ceremony. Typically the colours are lodged in a church which has a strong connection with the Regiment. This will usually be the principal church in the County Town or city where the Regiment recruited. The Commando Association did have a flag created on which to display their battle honours and this was laid up in St Paul's Cathedral on 1st May 1971, in the presence of Queen Elizabeth the Queen Mother. I have a sound recording of the service which will be donated in my father's name to the National Army Museum.

** The majority of promotions granted to the commandos were temporary and subject to confirmation by the soldier's originating unit. This meant that the unit wasn't required to uphold them when the soldiers returned to their units after the war. Only promotions to commissioned rank had to be honoured, as they were granted by the War Office and signed personally by the King.

*My father's medals. L-R 1939-1945 Star, Africa Star, Italy Star, France and Germany Star, The Defence Medal, War Medal 1939-1945, General Service Medal with Malaya clasp.*

# Appendix A – Structure of a Commando

A traditional infantry battalion is made up of a hierarchical structure:

- A Section is eight men, led by a Corporal.
- A Platoon is made up of four sections, commanded by a subaltern (Second Lieutenant, Lieutenant or Captain. The Captain would be 2$^{nd}$ in command of the company) with a Sergeant as his second in command.
- A Company is made up of four platoons, commanded by a Major.
- A battalion is made up of four rifle companies and an HQ company, commanded by a Lieutenant Colonel, with a Major as his Second in Command.

The commando structured themselves differently, in order to be more of a 'flat' command structure.

Initially a Commando was made up of ten troops of forty seven men and three officers. It was split into two sections, with a Second Lieutenant or Lieutenant in command of each section and a Captain commanding the troop. The CO was a Lieutenant Colonel, with a Major as his second in command. Initially there was no HQ Troop as such, but another officer would be appointed as Quartermaster, responsible for providing equipment and making sure that the troops all had billets (accommodation in the civilian community) and there was a doctor and a padre in each commando.

This structure was found to be unwieldy in combat, so it was re-organised into six troops of sixty ORs and three officers. This was also a convenient number as a single troop could fit into two landing craft. Fifty men meant that there were either too few men in each craft, or that troops had to be split up in order to make best use of landing craft capacity.

By the time that Stan Scott joined 3 Commando, the role of each troop in 3 Commando had been clearly defined. 1, 4, 5 and 6 troops were called assault troops; 2 troop was heavy weapons and 3 Troop was designated as 'parachute trained' though, as mentioned in Chapter 10, the training was never completed. There was a small HQ Troop made up of quartermasters, signallers, medics, padre and drivers (when there was transport). However, when it came to combat the HQ Troop operated as assault troops like any other commando soldier (except for the medics and padre, who were 'non-combatants' under the terms of the Geneva Convention).

As discussed elsewhere, above Commando level, from 1943 onwards, the organisation consisted of four Special Service Brigades (later renamed Commando Brigades). 1$^{st}$ and 4$^{th}$ Special Service brigades operated in North West Europe, 2$^{nd}$ Special Service Brigade in Sicily and Italy and 3$^{rd}$ Special Service Brigade in Burma.

In North West Europe the Special Service Brigades were attached to divisions, after D Day it was 6$^{th}$ Airborne Division, but later it varied depending on where the brigade was employed.

A brigade is commanded by a Brigadier with a full Colonel as his second in command. A Division is commanded by a Major General.

At the higher levels of formation, two or more Divisions make up a Corps, commanded by a Lieutenant General and two or more Corps make up an Army, commanded by a full General. Two or more armies make up an Army Group and would be commanded by a Field Marshall.

At each level of a formation above the Commando (or battalion) there are additional resources available to the commander. These may include artillery, field hospitals, aircraft, combat engineers, mobile workshops and logistics units.

# Appendix B – The Commando Order

The infamous Commando Order or *Kommandobefehl* was issued on the instructions of Adolf Hitler on 18th October 1942 and stated that all commandos/special forces personnel who were captured, even those in uniform, were to be executed without trial. This followed a raid on Sark (Operation Basalt, see Appendix C) which resulted in four out of five German prisoners being killed by commandos, allegedly while trying to escape to raise the alarm. The fifth prisoner was taken back to England.

The order was that any captured commando was to be handed over to the *Sicherheitsdeinst* (SD - Security Service) who would carry out the executions, but the *Schutzstaffel* (SS – the paramilitary wing of the Nazi party) also carried out executions. Other branches of the German armed forces found the order distasteful and not in keeping with the rules of war, so they tended to record the units from which prisoners came in accordance with their cap badges, rather than identifying them as commandos. This dischord between the Commando Order and the rules of war was adequately demonstrated by the paratroop commander at Malati Bridge, who really didn't want to hand Erskine and his sergeant over to the SS officer.

There is a school of thought that suggests that Hitler gave the order because he had become enraged by the effect that the commando raids were having on his forces. He is known to have described the commandos and other special forces as nothing more than thugs and gangsters. It is suggested, therefore, that the Sark raid was only a pretext for an order that would have been issued anyway. Even if this view is not correct, ordering the execution of enemy personnel without benefit of trial is regarded as a war crime (just one of many on a very long list).

Only twelve written copies of the order were ever made, which suggests that the German High Command were not comfortable with the legality of the order. Outside of those twelve copies the order was disseminated by word of mouth alone.

As for the commandos themselves, their morale was given a mighty boost by the knowledge that their actions had so enraged Hitler and were having such an impact that he had thought the Commando Order necessary. It also gave them greater determination to fight on against seemingly insuperable odds, knowing that a death sentence might result from their surrender. The commandos always understood the risks they were taking and few regretted volunteering.

This is a list of known occassions when Allied personnel were executed under the Commando Order:

- The first victims were two officers and five other ranks of Operation Musketoon (Glomfjord, Norway), who were shot in Sachsenhausen on the morning of 23rd October 1942.

- In November 1942, British survivors of Operation Freshman (Telemark, Norway) were executed.

- In December 1942, Royal Marine commandos captured during Operation Frankton (Bordeaux, France) were executed under this order. After the captured Royal Marines were executed by a naval firing squad in Bordeaux, the Commander of the Navy Admiral Erich Raeder wrote in the *Seekriegsleitung* war diary that the executions of the Royal Marines were something "new in international law since the soldiers were wearing uniforms".

- On 30th July 1943, the captured seven-man crew of the Royal Norwegian Navy motor torpedo boat *MTB 345* were executed by the Germans in Bergen, Norway on the basis of the Commando Order.

- January 1944 British Lt. William A. Millar escaped from Colditz Castle and vanished; it is speculated he was captured and killed in a Concentration Camp.

- In March 1944, 15 soldiers of the U.S. Army, including two officers, landed on the Italian coast as part of an OSS operation code-named Ginny II. They were captured and executed.

- After the Normandy landings, 34 SAS soldiers and a USAAF pilot were captured during Operation Bullbasket (Poitiers, France) and executed. Most were shot, but three were killed by lethal injection while recovering from wounds in hospital.

- In September 1944 seven British Commandos (along with 40 Dutch members of Englandspiel) were executed over two days at Mauthausen concentration camp, Austria.

- On 21 November 1944 US airman and prisoner of war Lt. Americo S. Galle was executed at Enschede, Holland by SS Unterscharführer Herbert Germoth by order of SS General Karl Eberhard Schöngarth.

- On 9th December 1944, five US airmen of the 20th Bombardment Squadron were captured and executed near Kaplitz, Czechoslovakia. Franz Strasser was tried and executed on 10 December 1945 for participation in the murders.

- On 27th December 1944, US airman and prisoner of war Lt. Lester J. Epstein was captured near Bastogne, Belgium. His shallow grave was found in January 1945; his head had been smashed in by rifle butts.

- Between October 1944 and March 1945, nine men of the United States Army Air Corps were summarily executed after being shot down and captured in Jurgen Stroop's district. Their known names were Sergeant Willard P. Perry, Sergeant Robert W. Garrison, Private Ray R. Herman, Second Lieutenant William A. Duke, Second Lieutenant Archibald B. Monroe, Private Jimmie R. Heathman, Lieutenant William H. Forman, and Private Robert T. McDonald. When Moczarski reminded him that the killing of POWs was defined as criminal under the Hague and Geneva Conventions, Stroop responded, "It was common knowledge that American flyers were terrorists and murderers who used methods contrary to civilized norms ... We were given a statement to that effect from the highest authorities. It was accompanied by an order from Heinrich Himmler." As a result, he explained, all nine POWs had been taken to the forest and given "a ration of lead for their American necks".

- On 24th January 1945, nine OSS men, including Lt. Holt Green of the Dawes mission (Slovakia), others of the Houseboat mission, four British SOE agents, and AP war correspondent Joseph Morton, were shot at Mauthausen by SS Hauptsturmführer Georg Bachmayer on orders of Ernst Kaltenbrunner. Joseph Morton was the only Allied correspondent to be executed by the Axis during World War II.

- In 1945, Lt. Jack Taylor USNR and the Dupont mission (Austria) were captured by the men of Gestapo agent Johann Sanitzer. Sanitzer asked the RSHA for instructions on a possible deal that Taylor proposed, but Kaltenbrunner's staff reminded him "of Hitler's edict that all captured officers attached to foreign missions were to be executed". Taylor was convicted of espionage, though he claimed to be an ordinary soldier. He was sent to Mauthausen. He survived, barely, but gathered evidence, and was eventually a witness at the war crimes trials.

- On 13th February 1945, eight survivors of a B-17 crash in Austria were captured; four survived the war and four were executed.

# Appendix C – Commando Operations of World War II

In this book I have concentrated almost exclusively on the exploits of 3 Commando, but there were, at one time, thirteen Army commandos (numbered 1 – 12 and 14, the number 13 wasn't used) raised in the UK and a further three in the Middle East theatre (50, 51 and 52 (Middle East) Commandos). From 1942 onwards the Royal Marines founded another eight commandos and there were specialist units such as 30 Commando, the Royal Engineers Commando and the Royal Navy Beach Commando. It is fitting that their operations should also be remembered.

10 (Inter-Allied) Cdo (10 (IA) Cdo) was made up of soldiers who had escaped from the various countries of occupied Europe. There were two troops of French, one Dutch, one Belgian, one Norwegian, one Polish and one Yugoslavian. X Troop was made up of several nationalities, but they were all German speaking and many were Jewish. Generally speaking, the troop(s) taking part in an operation would be from the country where the operation took place, eg Operation Infatuate used the Dutch troop from 10 (IA) Cdo. They were also used extensively as guides and interpreters in operations such as Claymore and Archery.

12 Cdo were drawn from Northern Irish regiments, but it was disbanded in late 1943 and its troops dispersed, mainly to 1, 5 and 6 Cdos. 14 Cdo were established specifically for operations in Norway, but were disbanded in late 1943 as the focus of the war effort shifted to Italy and France. The ski troop of 14 Commando was retained until the end of the war.

Below is a list of all the operations in which the commandos took part, arranged in alphabetical order. Details, some sketchy but some fuller, of most of these operations can be found on the Commando Veterans' Association website, listed against the commando(s) that carried it out. This list doesn't include the periods of combat operations when the commandos fought as part of larger formations, such as 3 Commando's time in 1945 when they returned to the front line in the wake of the Battle Of The Bulge.

Dates, where given, are the starting dates of the operation only. Some operations lasted a day, some lasted several weeks. Where troops embarked on landing craft or ships the night before an operation, I have tried to give the date of the actual landing.

While I have tried to capture all known operations, there may be some smaller ones that I have missed and I apologise for those omissions.

**Abercrombie;** 21st April 1942; Hardelot, France; 4 Cdo.

**Addition;** 19th April 1941; Bardia, Libya; 7 Cdo.

**Ambassador;** 14th July 1940; Guernsey; 3 Cdo and 11 Independent Company (who later became part of 1 Cdo).

**Anklet;** 26th December 1941; Lofotoen Island, Norway; 12 Cdo.

**Aquatint;** 11th September 1942; Normandy (what would later be called Omaha Beach); Small Scale Raiding Force.

**Archery;** 27th Decmber 1941; Vågsøy and Måløy, Norway; 3 Cdo plus elements of 2, 4 and 6 Cdos.

**Avalanche;** 9th September 1943; Salerno, Italy; 2 Cdo as part of the Salerno landings.

**Barricade;** 14th August 1942; Barfleur, Normandy; Small Scale Raiding Force.

**Basalt;** 3rd October 1942; Sark, Channel Islands; elements of 12 Cdo and the Small Scale Raiding Force.

**Batman;** November 1942; Cherbourg, France; elements of 12 Cdo.

**Battle of Hill 170;** 31st January 1945; Kangaw, Myanmar (Burma); 1 Cdo, 5 Cdo, 42 (RM) Cdo.

**Bean;** 23rd November 1944; Maungdaw, Myanmar (Burma); 1 Cdo plus elements of 5 Cdo.

**Biting;** 27th February 1942; Bruneval, Normandy; 12 Cdo (recovering paratroops who had attacked a German radar station).

**Bizerte;** 1st December 1942; Tunisia; 1 Cdo.

**Blackcock;** 14th January 1945: Roermond, The Netherlands; 3 Cdo, 45 (RM) Cdo.

**Bottle;** 13th October 1945, Pak Shek Chau, China; 1 Cdo. *

**Branford;** 7th September 1942; Burhou, Channel islands; Small Scale Raiding Force.

**Bristle;** 3rd June 1942; Boulogne and Le Touquet, France; 11 Independent Company Company (who later became part of 1 Cdo), Small Scale Raiding Force. The first commando raid.

**Cartoon;** 24th January 1943; Leirvik, Norway; elements of 12 Cdo.

**Carey;** 12th April 1943; various Norwegian Fjords; 12 Cdo.

**Cauldron;** 19th August 1942; Dieppe, France; 4 Cdo and elements of 10 (IA) Cdo as part of Operation Jubilee.

**Chariot;** 28th March 1942; St Nazaire, France; 2 Cdo plus elements from 1, 3, 4, 5, 9 and 12 cdo's.

**Checkmate;** 28th April 1943; Kopervik, Norway; 14 Cdo.

**Chess;** 27th July 1941; Ambleteuse, France; 12 Cdo.

**Chopper;** 28th September 1941; Luc Sur Mer, France; 1 Cdo.

**Claymore;** 4th March 1941; Lofoten Islands; 3 Cdo, 4 Cdo.

**Crackers;** 23rd February 1943; Sognefjord, Norway; elements of 10 (IA) Cdo, 12 Cdo, 14 Cdo, 30 Cdo.

**Darlington;** 24th May 1944; Italy; 9 Cdo.

**Detained I;** 18th March 1944; Solta, Croatia; 2 Cdo, 43 (RM) Cdo.

**Detained II;** 8th May 1944; Solta, Croatia; 2 Cdo.

**Detained III;** 17th September 1944; Solta, Croatia; 43 (RM) Cdo.

**Devon;** 3rd October 1943; Termoli, Italy; 3 Cdo, 40 (RM) Cdo.

**Dryad;** 2nd September 1942; Casquets Lighthouse, Channel islands; Small Scale Raiding Force.

**Exporter;** 8th June 1941; Litani River, Syria; 11 Cdo.

**Fahrenheit;** 12th December 1942; Pointe de Plouezec, France; elements of 12 Cdo.

**Ferdy;** 8th September 1943; Porto San Venere (now known as Vibo Valentia), Italy; 40 (RM) Cdo and elements of 3 Cdo.

**Flipper;** 14th November 1941; Beda Littoria, Libya; 11 Cdo.

**Flodden;** 19th August 1942; Dieppe, France; 3 Cdo as part of Operation Jubilee.

**Flounced;** 2nd June 1944; Brac, Croatia; elements of 40 (RM) Cdo and 43 (RM) Cdo.

**Floxo;** 28th October 1944; Dubrovnik, Croatia; 43 (RM) Cdo.

**Forfar;** 4th July – 4th September 1943; Pas de Calais, France; elements of 10 (IA) Cdo and 12 Cdo; a series of six raids to suggest an invasion was imminent..

**Foxrock;** 31st May 1942; St Valerie en Caux, France; 12 Cdo.

**Hardtack;** 25th – 27th December 1943; Channel Islands and Northern France; 10 (IA) Cdo and 12 Cdo. Several simultaneous raids to suggest an invasion was imminent..

**Healing II;** 29th July 1944; Spilje, Albania; 2 Cdo, elements of 9 Cdo and 40 (RM) Cdo.

**Horse;** 14th Januray 1945; Noord-Brabant, The Netherlands; 47 (RM) Cdo, 10 (IA) Cdo.

**Huckaback;** 27th February 1942; Herm, Channel Islands; Small Sclae Raiding Force.

**Husky;** 10th July 1943; Sicily; 2 Cdo, 3 Cdo, 40 (RM) Cdo, 41 (RM) Cdo and Royal Navy Beach Cdo, as part of the invasion of Sicily.

**Infatuate;** 1st November 1944; Walcheren, The Netherlands; 4 Cdo, elements of 10 (IA) Cdo, 41, 47 and 48 (RM) Cdos, Royal Navy Beach Cdo.

**Ironclad;** 5th May 1942; Diego Suarez, Madagascar; 5 Cdo.

**Jubilee:** 19th August 1942; Dieppe, France; 40 (RM) Cdo, 30 Cdo.

**Kitbag;** 9th December 1941; Florø, Norway; elements of 6 and 12 Cdos. Aborted before landing following the accidental explosion of a grenade.

**Mercerised;** 22nd September 1944; Sarande, Albania; 2 Cdo, 40 (RM) Cdo.

**Messina to Palermo Railway;** 29th/30th August 1941; Sicily; 2 Cdo.

**Musketoon;** 11th September 1942; Glomfjuord, Norway; elements of 2 Cdo and 10 (IA) Cdo.

**Myrmidon;** 2nd April 1942; Adour Estuary; France; 1 Cdo, 6 Cdo. Aborted before landing after one of the ships ran aground on a sand bar.

**Operation X;** 19th March 1944; Anzio, Italy; 9 Cdo.

**Overlord**: 6th June 1944; Normandy, France; 3, 4, 6, 10 (IA) Cdos, 30 Cdo Assualt Unit; 41, 45, 46, 47 and 48 (RM) Cdos, Royal Navy Beach Commando; as part of the Allied invasion of France.

**Paddle;** 16th August 1944; Normandy, France; 1st and 4th Special Service Brigades; the eastwards breakout from the Normandy beachheads.

**Partridge;** 29th December 1943; Garigliano River, Italy; 9 Cdo.

**Pound;** 3rd September 1942; Ushant Peninsula, Brittany; 12 Cdo plus US Rangers.

**Premium;** 27th February 1942; Wassenaar, The Netherlands; 10 (IA) Cdo.

**Rearguard Action on Crete;** 26th May 1941; Crete; 7 Cdo, 50, 51 (Middle East) Cdos.

**Roast;** 1st April 1945; Commachio, Italy; 2 and 9 Cdos, 40 and 43 (RM) Cdos, Special Boat Service.

**Screwdriver;** 11th March 1944; Alethangyaw, Myanmar (Burma); 44 (RM) Cdo, 5 Cdo.

**Shingle**; 3rd March 1944; Anzio, Italy; 9 Cdo as part of the Anzio landings.

**Silchar;** 15th April 1944; Assam, India; 5 Cdo, 44 (RM) Cdo.

**Sunstar;** 23rd November 1941; Houlgate, France; 9 Cdo.

**Torch**; 8th November 1942; Algiers; 1 Cdo, 6 Cdo, as part of the Allied invasion of Morroco, Algeria and Tunisia.

**Widgeon**; 23rd March 1945; Wesel, Germany; 3 and 6 Cdos, 45 and 46 (RM) Cdos. The crossing of the River Rhein.

Operation names were allocated in alphabetical order from a list published at the start of each year. Once a name had been used it wasn't used again, though some operations, such as Detained, might have several phases carrying the same code name but with a suffix numeral for each phase. Once the letter Z had been used, a new list was started at A.

* The war was over by this time and this operation may be seen as a policing action.

# Appendix D – Commando VCs

Given the nature of their duties, it is unsurprising that the commandos garnered more than their fair share of medals and awards during World War II. Among them were eight Victoria Crosses. Below is a list of the eight recipients. The list is in alphabetical order.

**Sergeant T F Durrant VC;** 27th/28th March 1942; Operation Chariot; 1 Cdo. Refused to leave his Lewis gun on board a motor launch, despite being wounded. Posthumous.

**Lance Corporal H E Harden VC**; 23rd January 1945; Operation Blackcock; 45 (RM) Cdo; While wounded himself, he attempted to rescue three wounded commandos. Posthumous.

**Corporal T P Hunter VC**; 3rd April 1945; Operation Roast; 43 (RM) Cdo; Single handedly captured a house, forcing the surrender of six Germans, then offered himself as a target to cover the advance of the rest of his troop. Posthumous.

**Major G C T Keyes VC MC.**; 18th November 1942; 11 Cdo. Operation Flipper. Leading an operation two hundred and fifty miles behind enemy lines in North Africa. Posthumous.

**Lieutenant G A Knowland VC**; 31st January 1945; Kangaw, Burma; 1 Cdo; Held the enemy at bay with Bren gun and mortar fire while standing fully exposed to return fire. Posthumous.

**Major A F E V Shau Lassen VC** (Danish National); 9th April 1945; Operation Roast; Special Boat Service attached to 2 Cdo Brigade; Aggressive leadership against superior numbers to capture enemy positions. Posthumous.

**Lieutenant Colonel A C Newman VC**; 27th/28th March 1942. Operation Chariot; 2 Cdo; Leading his commando at St Nazaire.

**Lieutenant P A Porteus VC**; 19th August 1942; Operation Cauldron; 4 Cdo; Having been wounded, he attacked his assailant and killed him with his own bayonet, then crossed open ground under heavy fire before leading a charge to capture the enemy position.

For more details of how these awards were won, or to view the full Roll of Honour for the wartime commandos, please visit the Commando Veterans Association website:

**http://www.commandoveterans.org/CommandoVC**
**http://www.commandoveterans.org/commando_roll_of_honour_WW2**

On war memorials, commandos killed during World War II are normally listed against the regiment or corps in which they originally enlisted, rather than against their commando number. The same applies to the dedications on their graves in Commonwealth War Cemeteries, where their regimental badge is also engraved on the headstone.

# Appendix E – A Short History Of The Middlesex Regiment

The Middlesex Regiment started out as two regiments of the foot soldiers, the 57th and 77th. The 57th were raised in 1755 as the 51st Regiment, but were renumbered in 1756. In 1782 they became the 57th (West Middlesex) Regiment of Foot. This gave them the right to recruit soldiers on the western side of the county of Middlesex, without fear of competition from other regiments. This area included such boroughs as Hammersmith and Fulham which would eventually be absorbed into Greater London. The 77th were raised in 1787 as a regiment of East India Company soldiers recruited from Britain and Ireland. On returning to England in 1807, after being absorbed into the regular army, they were designated the 77th (East Middlesex) Regiment of Foot. Like their neighbours, the West Middlesex, they were entitled to recruit from the eastern side of the county. This area included towns such as Enfield, Edmonton, Tottenham and Barnet, all of which would also eventually become part of Greater London.

It is from the 77th that the regiment earned the right to incorporate the Prince of Wales feathers and the motto "Ich Dein" (I serve) into their cap badge.

From the 57th Regiment the Middlesex earned their nickname the Die Hards. In 1811, at the Battle of Albuhera on the Iberian Peninsula, their mortally wounded Commanding Officer, Lieutenant Colonel William Inglis, exhorted his men to "die hard the 57th, die hard" as they battled against superior numbers of Napoleon's army.

A further tradition from the same battle was adopted from the 57th, that of the silent toast. After the battle the surviving officers are said to have melted down some of their silver accoutrements to make a cup. They and the NCO's of the battalion then passed the cup from hand to hand as each man present silently toasted the "immortal memory" of those that had fallen. The cup still exists and has the medal of the battle's longest living survivor, Colour Sergeant Henry

Holloway, mounted within it. At the Battle of Albuhera Henry Holloway was an 11 year old drummer boy.

The links to the now defunct county of Middlesex were re-asserted by the 1881 army reforms which joined the two regiments together and gave them the title of Duke of Cambridge's Own (Middlesex Regiment), which was to become The Middlesex Regiment (Duke of Cambridge's Own).

The Middlesex Regiment became a designated machine gun regiment as part of the Machine Gun Corps in 1915, when it was thought that infantry battalions weren't getting the best out of their machine guns. They were cumbersome and difficult to move, which discouraged their use in an advance and they were often abandoned during a retreat. The Vickers machine guns were replaced at battalion level by the less cumbersome Lewis gun and, from 1938 onwards, by the Bren gun. The Middlesex Regiment gave up their machine gun role and reverted to infantry duties after World War II.

During World War I the Middlesex Regiment grew to a total of forty nine battalions. Thirteen of these were Pals battalions, groups of men who volunteered en-mass to join the Army in response to Lord Kitchener's famous "Your County Needs You" appeal. Amongst these Pals battalions in the Middlesex Regiment were the Football Pals, professional footballers who joined up to set an example to their fans. Of course, not all of these pals were from the county of Middlesex. Most of these forty nine war time battalions weren't specialist machine gun units.

During the First World War the soldiers of the Middlesex Regiment won five Victoria Crosses. The combined battalions suffered in excess of twelve thousand casualties.

During World War II the Middlesex Regiment grew to twelve battalions, all of which served as specialist machine gun units. The 2nd Battalion were part of the British Expeditionary Force sent to France at the outbreak of the war and were involved in the retreat to Dunkirk. The 1st Battalion were in Hong Kong where the whole battalion was taken prisoner by the Japanese when they captured the colony on 25th December 1941. Many were killed when a ship the prisoners were being transported in, the Lisbon Maru, was sunk by the submarine USS Grouper on 1st October 1942. Many more died at the hands of the Japanese while prisoners of war.

The Regiment's Depot was at Inglis Barracks, Mill Hill, now part of the London Borough of Barnet. The regiment recruited from the heavily populated areas of North and West London, as well as from the smaller towns and villages of the county. Following the disbandment of the regiment the barracks was home to the British Forces Post Office (BFPO) until they moved to new accommodation at RAF Northolt in 2007. The Barracks has now been sold off for redevelopment. All that remains to mark its existence are three street names; Inglis Way, Guardhouse Way and Peninsular Close. The naming of Royal Engineers Way commemorates the years when the barracks was home to the BFPO.

The county of Middlesex itself disappeared under local government reforms of 1965 and was mainly swallowed up by the neighbouring London boroughs, with some towns being absorbed into Hertfordshire and Surrey.

Under a reorganisation that took place in 1966 the Middlesex Regiment became the 4th Battalion of the Queens Regiment, joined by The Queen's Royal Surrey Regiment, The Queens Own Buffs (The Royal Kent Regiment) and The Royal Sussex Regiment. A further reorganisation in 1992 saw the Queens Regiment combine with the Royal Hampshire Regiment to become the Princess of Wales Royal Regiment (Queens and Royal Hampshires), the title by which they are known today. Albuhera Day, the anniversary of the battle on 16th May 1811, is still a significant day for the regiment, when the silent toast is still drunk.

The colours of the Middlesex Regiment are laid up in The Chapel of St Erkenwald and St Ethelburga, St Paul's Cathedral. This chapel is also known as the Middlesex Regiment Chapel.

Artefacts belonging to the Middlesex Regiment are in the collection of the National Army Museum, Royal Hospital Road, Chelsea, London, SW3 4HT.

*Cap badge of the Middlesex Regiment*

For a more comprehensive history of the Regiment I recommend the book "The Middlesex Regiment (Duke of Cambridge's Own) (The 57th and 77th of Foot)" by Gregory Blaxland.

# Photographic Credits

## Dedication Page

Sgt Bob Cubitt (circa 1952) - Cubitt family collection.

## Chapter 1

Harry and Charlotte Cubitt – Cubitt family collection.
10 Shorrolds Road – Cubitt family collection.

## Chapter 2

Shortly after joining up, 1938 – Cubitt family collection.
Dad's certificate of training as a cook dated 1941 – Cubitt family collection.
Photo credit: (H17472, B5103, H26620). - reproduced under licence from the Imperial War Museum. Licence no LIC-16982-R8C0Z7

## Chapter 3

Photo credit: (H17472, B5103, H26620). - reproduced under licence from the Imperial War Museum. Licence no LIC-16982-R8C0Z7
November Sun at The Memorial – with the kind permission of the Commando Veterans Association.
Fairbairn Sykes Fighting Knife – Cubitt family collection.
Commando shoulder badge featuring the Sykes-Fairbairn Fighting Knife – with the kind permission of the Commando Veterans Association.

## Chapter 5

The Combined Operations shoulder patch - with the kind permission of the Commando Veterans Association.
Commandos wounded at Vågsøy – with the kind permission of the Evening Express.
The Vågsøy/Måløy Memorial – with the kind permission of www.bunkerpictures.nl

## Chapter 6

Soldiers of 3 Commando on their return from Dieppe - with the kind permission of the Commando Veterans Association.
3 Commando bathing party in Lewes, September 1944 – Cubitt family collection.
The cliffs at Berneval le Grand – with the kind permission of Nick Cooper.
The memorial to 3 Commando at Berneval le Grand – with the kind permission of the Commando Veterans Association.

## Chapter 7

Commandos on the roof of a train – Cubitt family collection.

## Chapter 8

Lieutenant John Channon Erskine - with the kind permission of the Commando Veterans Association.
Malati Bridge - The pill box seized by Erskine and his men - with the kind permission of the Commando Veterans Association.
3 Commando commemoration stone - with the kind permission of the Commando Veterans Association.

## Chapter 9

HQ Troop, 3 Commando, 1943 – Cubitt family collection.
Jack Cox - with the kind permission of the Commando Veterans Association.

## Chapter 10

Stan "Scotty" Scott in 1945 - with the kind permission of the Commando Veterans Association.
Photo credit: D Day, ©Imperial War Museum (H 39038A and H 39041). - reproduced under licence from the Imperial War Museum. Licence no LIC-19374-K5Q5C0
3 Commando members in Normandy – Cubitt family collection.

## Chapter 11

Ardennes – my Dad and other 3 Cdo members hitching a lift with some Americans – Cubitt family collection.

## Chapter 12

Daily Mirror article – reproduced with the kind permission from the Daily Mirror.
Malaya 1954 – Dad is front row, 3rd from the left – Cubitt family collection.
My Father's Medals – Cubitt Family Collection

## Appendices

Cap badge of the Middlesex Regiment – Cubitt family collection.

# Bibliography

In alphabetical order:

Castle Commando; Donald Gilchrist; West Highland Museum Publishing; 1960.

Commando; Brigadier John Durnford-Slater DSO & Bar; Greenhill Books, New Edition; 2002.

Commando Veterans Association, The.
**http://www.commandoveterans.org/**

Fighting With The Commandos: The Recollections of Stan Scott No 3 Commando; Edited by Neil Barber; Pen and Sword Books ltd; 2008.

Green Beret, The; Hilary St George Saunders; Michael Joseph, 1949.

The Vaagso Raid; Joseph H Devins jr; The Chilton Book Company, 1968.

Real History of World War II, The: A New Look At The Past; Alan Axelrod; Stirling Publishing & Co Inc; 2008.

Storm From The Sea; Peter Young; Greenhill Books; New Edition; 2002.

For more information on both the Army Commandos and the Royal Marine Commandos, including the first-hand accounts of veterans, from 1940 through to the present day, visit the Commando Veterans Association website: **http://www.commandoveterans.org/**

# Accessing the Military Records of Relatives

Under the Data Protection Act 1998, former service personnel may ask for copies of their own service records. After their death, the relatives of former service personnel are also entitled to ask for copies of their service records. Former service personnel or their next of kin may apply for copies free of charge, but other relatives have to pay a fee of £30 (at time of writing).

The following link provides more information and downloadable forms which can be used to apply.

**https://www.gov.uk/get-copy-military-service-records/apply-for-your-own-records**

# And Now

As this book has focused on the exploits of 3 Commando, many stories of the bravery exhibited in other commandos haven't been told and even some of the stories about 3 Commando have appeared in a very cursory form. For this reason, the author has embarked on a new fiction series that has been inspired by the exploits of the Army Commandos. The series will be called "Carter's Commandos", after their fictional leading character and follows a route around Europe not dissimilar to that taken by 3 Commando.

Both the author Robert Cubitt and Selfishgenie Publishing hope that you have enjoyed reading this book.

Please tell your friends about it, or write a review on Amazon or mention it on your favourite social networking site.

For further titles that may be of interest to you please visit the

Ex-L-Ence website at selfishgenie.com

Printed in Great Britain
by Amazon

40233586R00116